The Throne of David

Christ's 5-Point Plan for Building His Church

Dr. Charles R. Vogan Jr.

Copyright © 2006 Charles R. Vogan Jr.
All rights reserved

Scripture taken from the HOLY BIBLE, NEW INTERNATIONAL VERSION, Copyright © 1973, 1978, 1984 International Bible Society. Used by permission of Zondervan Bible Publishers.

ISBN 978-0-6151-3860-2

Ravenbrook Publishers

A subsidiary of
Shenandoah Bible Ministries

www.shenbible.org

Contents

Introduction — 5

Part One

    Chaos — 9

    David's plan — 24

    The Mission — 35

Part Two

    A King in Heaven — 57

    War Mode — 76

    God-centered Ministry — 97

    Government — 116

    Service — 137

Conclusion — 157

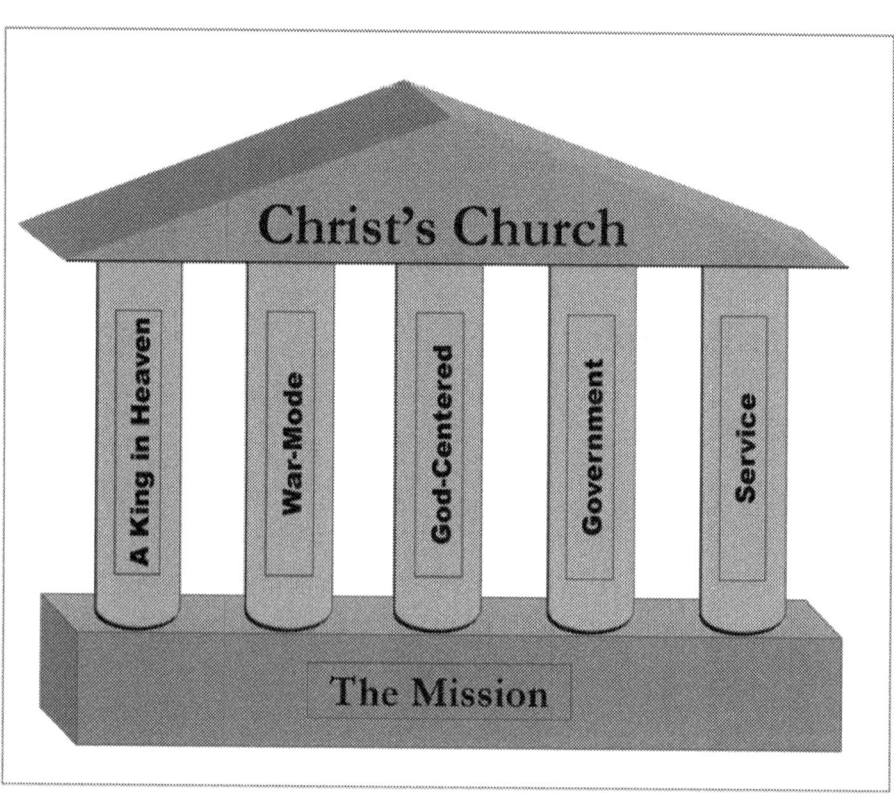

Introduction

In the Book of Revelation, Jesus addresses seven churches in Asia Minor about their performance. Whether you take these seven churches as representative of all churches since that time, or symbolic of the Church Age in general, there are a few obvious points here that we shouldn't miss.

First, the criterion is not what churches and members think about their performance. What matters is what Jesus thinks about them. He is the Head of the Church, the King of kings. In his hands are all authority and power. Our Mission is to meet his requirements for church work. Those churches that don't care what Jesus thinks – they are only doing what they want to do – he will shut them down. They are of no use to him. This fact ought to send us continually to the throne in Heaven to find out, first, what our duties really are, and second, whether we are, in his judgment, fulfilling that Mission.

Second, there's room for improvement in every church. Jesus had some hard things to say to most of the Asia Minor churches. The two that he didn't have anything negative to say about still had room for improvement. This means that there is no perfect church – not in this world. This means also that, as you look around in your church with spiritual "glasses" that Christ's Spirit provides, you will see sins, failures, ignorance, willfulness, rebellion, materialism, self-centeredness, hardness of heart – in fact all the sins of the world transferred into the four walls of your assembly. There is always a lot of work to do.

Third – and this follows from the previous point – we must *change*. When a church gets so smug and set in its ways that it continues Sunday after Sunday in the same routine, never improving, never changing, thinking that it has arrived at the perfect setup – it has lost its sense of

Introduction

mission. It is dead. Like a living body, the church is a changing organism on many levels in order to maintain life. A church that isn't changing in real ways – in ways that the Lord Jesus demands change – is a dead body. And unfortunately adults really, really hate to change anything that they're already satisfied with. Which means that most churches today have little chance of becoming what Jesus wants them to be.

But change is risky if you don't have a solid plan. Our culture is all too willing to change even the church into its image: they want the freedom to throw away God's rules and invent their own. They want free, unbridled lust and power. Even within the church, there are many (conflicting!) opinions on what the church should become, and they look disturbingly like the world we live in.

What we need is God's assessment – his Truth that clears up the confusion and chaos. The Son of God has definite goals in mind for any and every church of his. A living, spiritually healthy church is going to be a distressing reality to the sinful world, but it will be able to heal the sickness of the world – directly for those who are part of its life, and indirectly as it faithfully and fearlessly confronts the world's wickedness.

The time has come to listen to what Jesus has to say to his churches.

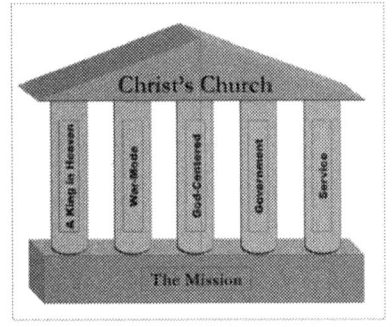

Part One

Chaos

In those days Israel had no king; everyone did as he saw fit.
(Judges 21:25)

When the Israelites entered the Promised Land under Joshua, they had just come through an amazing series of events that started with the Exodus from Egypt. They had all witnessed the power and majesty of their God, leading them through the Wilderness from miracle to miracle. Not a man among them could claim that he never experienced the blessing of God's hand upon him in their hour of trial.

But after a generation or two in Canaan, the people forgot about God. Life was good, temptations to sin were real and present, and it proved to be too difficult to take a spiritual God – a God they couldn't see or hear – very seriously. So when they drifted away from God's presence, and his rule over them, they naturally fell into chaos on an individual and national level. In short, Israel turned into a national disaster. They worshiped false gods, they lived in the immorality of their pagan neighbors, they lusted after the pleasures and treasures of this world. And even though they "cried out to the Lord in their distress," the short reprieve that God granted them under each of the Judges didn't last long. The problem was that they didn't know how to live with a God they couldn't see. Or, could we say that it was just a little *too* easy to live without him!

In the spirit of the Book of Revelation, we should take a hard look at our churches today. Through the eyes of Christ – we have his Word to guide us here – we can see the same signs of chaos in our ranks. Any way you look at it, the church in our society is a disaster. I can't help but think that this situation exists because Jesus himself isn't here, in person, in the flesh, in his imposing presence, keeping us on track. We too are dealing with a King that we can't see. Not that this excuses us any more than it did the Israelites. They were required to walk by faith before their very real God; we are too. The fact that they came up with a thousand aberrations from the standards that God laid down for them only points out their distance from God; our present state of confusion points out our distance from him too.

If Jesus were really the Head of the Church, and we were all doing his will perfectly, we wouldn't be in the state we are in now. Anybody who knows Christ would have to admit that. He would be fixing the problems among us, bringing unity into the ranks, training us for battle, dictating our every move, and preparing us for the next world. We would all be part of *one* church. Instead, what we have are the following situations.

- **Denominations** – The curse within the modern church is the never-ending spirit of backbiting, fighting, divisions, envy and jealousy, one-upsmanship, competition, and hero worship that has gone on since the days of Paul. Remember that he complained about the Corinthians' tendency to line up behind their "favorite" leaders over against the others – as if God's servants were competing with each other for parts of the Kingdom!

> You are still worldly. For since there is jealousy and quarreling among you, are you not worldly? Are you not acting like mere men? For when one says, "I follow Paul," and another, "I follow Apollos," are you not mere men? What, after all, is Apollos? And what is Paul? Only servants, through whom you came to believe – as the Lord has assigned to each his task. I planted the seed, Apollos watered it, but God made it grow. So neither he who plants nor he who waters is anything, but only God, who makes things grow. The man who plants and the man who waters have one purpose, and each will be rewarded according to his own labor. For we are God's fellow workers; you are God's field, God's building. (1 Corinthians 3:3-9)

Church leaders actually encourage this attitude of splitting and divisions because it gives them an opportunity to rule over their own little kingdoms. Men love power. They love to dominate the lives of others. Instead of humbly working among the sheep that the Lord gave them, they build fortresses around "their" church to keep others out and to dictate to "their" people how to live – and they love how important all this makes them feel.

Many church splits and divisions happened because good men felt that the "mother church" was taking a wrong direction – doctrinally or politically – and the sheep shouldn't have to be forced against their will to go against God's plain commands. There should be another option besides staying with a corrupt church – hence, let's start a new church that will do it right.

That's difficult to argue against. It's true that you can have ignorant or even sinister people leading church members down the wrong road, and one must deal with that situation. But for many of us, our natures are just too militant to build a House of Peace. Like certain heathen religions, our solution to most problems is to start shooting each other! We argue, fight, back-stab, grab control, insist on our own way, etc. Most of the reasons that people have for fighting within the church are bad ones. They claim the right to split for the sake of purity, but their actual reasons for leaving the fellowship are paltry and pathetic.

Our battles should be against the churches' true enemies – not brothers! There are two kinds of truth: primary and secondary. The primary truths are what make us Christian in our religion, over against the beliefs of other religions. The secondary truths are still true, and important, but are like differences in the same family. We may have sharp differences with one another; but that doesn't mean that we can therefore leave the family.

Our unity is not based upon our agreement on every point of doctrine; it's grounded on the work of the Spirit of Christ making us part of God's family. You may not *like* the person you're sitting next to in church; but if he also believes that "Jesus Christ has come in the flesh" (1 John 4:2), then you are required to *love* him. (1 John 2:9-10) The primary doctrine brings us unity in Christ; the secondary doctrine reduces the friction between brothers.

We are not promoting the idea of "one world religion" here. We are reminding ourselves of the Early Church. Just the phrase "Early

Church" gives us the picture of Christians in all walks of life, in different locations, all sharing the same common faith in Christ. There was one church in those days.

> Make every effort to keep the unity of the Spirit through the bond of peace. There is one body and one Spirit – just as you were called to one hope when you were called – one Lord, one faith, one baptism; one God and Father of all, who is over all and through all and in all. (Ephesians 4:3-6)

And even those who glory in their own denominational distinctives are usually thrilled when they touch base with another believer halfway around the world in a strange context, someone with a different culture, using a different way to worship God. Their openness to a brother *there* exposes their judgmental attitude *here* – it's nothing but hypocrisy.

Instead of the unity of the Early Church, in our day we have new denominations springing up everywhere in the spirit of division. It's easy to rally a group of people around a cause when there's an enemy in sight. The spirit of condemnation rules: that other church down the road is wrong, we can't fellowship with them, only we have the truth, and you will be saved through our ministry alone. They are saying things about their brothers in the faith that they shouldn't be saying; they are shutting them out of fellowship; they are refusing the possibility of spiritual refreshment in each other. It's as if our brothers in the faith are the enemy!

If only your church, out of a million churches in this world, is right – that means that the other 999,999 churches are wrong. Sorry, but that smacks of self-delusion based on false standards.

- **Conflicting interpretations of the Bible** – To the average believer in the pew, the Bible *is* very simple – because he only understands a small part of it. But that doesn't worry him much because he lets his pastor handle the difficult parts. Thus he believes exactly what he is told to believe, without having dug it out for himself. As a result he wouldn't know the truth if he saw it.

Chaos

Pastors however know very well that there is actually little agreement in church circles on what the Bible teaches. The many commentaries in their libraries prove that. And of course each denomination has its own commentaries that teach the Bible from their own perspective, and the theological schools have their differing representatives also. By the time you amass a library containing all the possible interpretations that people and ages have imposed on the message of the Bible, you have to wonder if they are all talking about the same book! Has there been this much disagreement about the message of any other book in history?

I realize that the Bible is a large book – around 1500 pages in average editions. But surely a book that God gave mankind for his spiritual good can't be beyond his ability to understand. Surely there must be a simple message for the problems of life, a message that anybody with a reasonable mind can grasp.

But again, the many factions of those who call themselves Christians have invented innumerable theories about the Bible's true message. Almost all of this, however, is due to hidden agendas and ulterior motives.

The biggest culprit in our day for the contradictory ways of interpreting the Bible is Liberalism. For the last two hundred years at least, there's been a determined attack against the Bible. Modern man has discovered, through science in particular, a new freedom and power over his world that the ancients never enjoyed. So why fear the "gods" of the world when you can run the world yourself? And the Bible is a thorn in their side, because it represents the "old" standard that "primitive" peoples of the past believed. It certainly doesn't allow a free lifestyle that our modern world makes so easy. So to remove the thorn, "experts" have been busy destroying the foundations of the Bible so that now only "ignorant" people would take it at face value.

Liberalism (which is the formal name for the wave of unbelief that has swept the Western world in the last two centuries) is a way, or method, of looking at the Bible – basically, it doesn't believe it. Liberals want to keep the name Christian, but they don't want the doctrine of Christianity. It's amazing what they don't believe! They have more in common with pagan religions than the faith that the Apostles once taught. They don't believe in miracles, they don't believe in prophecy, they don't believe that Moses and Daniel and Paul wrote the books that are attributed to them, they don't believe in blood atonement, they don't believe in the integrity of the Gospels – and therefore they don't believe that the Bible is the Word of God.

Yet in spite of this unbelief they still call themselves Christians! The reason is twofold: *first*, they want to be able to continue living in their sins without someone condemning them with God's Word against sinners. So they take great pains to explain away the doctrine and history of the Bible – if we can't depend on this ancient doctrine, if it has manuscript and culture problems, if it's just the words of men [and if so, why can't we rewrite it to suit ourselves?], then we don't have to take it so seriously. We can live as we please – that "sin" business is just your outdated attitude, not the "spirit" of the Bible's message. You need to be *relevant*, they tell us – not old-fashioned!

Second, there's a lot of money to be made in the service of the church. Would people actually be dishonest and use the Bible and the church as a vehicle to material gain? Absolutely! If they jumped to another religion they wouldn't have the opportunities they have under the church's umbrella. Life is good if you can stay in the church, come up with your own doctrines, enjoy the fruits of immorality, and get paid for it too! Paul knew about these kinds of parasites in the church.

> If anyone teaches false doctrines and does not agree to the sound instruction of our Lord Jesus Christ and to godly teaching, he is conceited and understands nothing. He has an unhealthy interest in controversies and quarrels about words that result in envy, strife, malicious talk, evil suspicions and constant friction between men of corrupt mind, who have been robbed of the truth *and who think that godliness is a means to financial gain*. (1 Timothy 6:3-5)

These are the hidden agendas of those who try to foist their unnatural and dishonest "interpretations" of the Bible on unsuspecting church members. The result has been complete chaos on the church scene for the last two hundred years; hardly anybody knows what to take seriously in the Bible anymore.

The reason that the "battle for the Bible" is so important is because the Bible claims to be *the only standard for doctrine and practice*. If this is true, then we need to believe what it says. If people can disprove that claim, then they will live and believe as they please.

- **People aren't cured of their sins** – You would expect people who have gone to church for many years to be holy saints. At the very least they ought to understand the problems and Mission of the church well enough to cooperate with God in the saving of their souls. Instead we see all the sins of the world still staining their hearts and minds. Seemingly the ministry of the Spirit has done nothing at all for them.

If you think that the members of your church are accomplished Christians, be careful. When we only see each other for about an hour every week – on Sunday morning – we can generally get along with each other. But let an issue come up that divides the feelings of the members and you will see all the latent animosity and hard-heartedness that is buried deep within people's hearts come out into the open. Politics (yes, there is politics in the church!) and disagreements over money will often bring it out.

And by nature people tend to cover over their embarrassing character traits. Of course we present ourselves as wonderful Christians at the church service; but follow us home and you will no doubt see things about us that we didn't want the whole public to know! It's amazing what sinners we truly are.

This means that whatever ministry that the church thinks it's providing for church members isn't really doing the job. It doesn't seem to change their hearts from sinners to saints, from nasty to nice, from self-centered to God-centered. In fact, current church ministries seem to be doing the opposite: they encourage people to hide their real selves at home and display a "holy" character in church gatherings. Instead of addressing the problem they are ignoring the problem. The church is actually growing hypocrites, not saints.

Chaos

The biggest reason for this alarming reversal is that we don't understand the true Mission of the church: it's supposed to be a spiritual hospital, not a convention of perfect people. It's for healing sinners, not for congratulating Pharisees. It's a perfect opportunity, in fact the only realistic opportunity in this fallen world, to identify sin, cleanse the heart and mind of its sickening and deadening powers, and restore the image of God in man. But until we put ourselves in this crisis mode – "we are here to solve the Problem" – the church experience isn't going to change a thing in us.

We have abundant reason for doubting the effectiveness of many churches. For example, why do so many pastors and church leaders fall to the baser sins of adultery, greed, lying, stealing and materialism that we find so often these days? Because the message that they teach didn't change their own hearts. Paul dreaded such a possibility.

> No, I beat my body and make it my slave so that after I have preached to others, I myself will not be disqualified for the prize. (1 Corinthians 9:27)

Why is there so much fighting and backbiting and gossip and animosity and even hatred within the walls of the church? Because all those sermons and Bible lessons failed to fill people's hearts full of peace and love toward the brethren.

> What causes fights and quarrels among you? Don't they come from your desires that battle within you? You want something but don't get it. You kill and covet, but you cannot have what you want. You quarrel and fight. You do not have, because you do not ask God. When you ask, you do not receive, because you ask with wrong motives, that you may spend what you get on your pleasures. (James 4:1-3)

> If you keep on biting and devouring each other, watch out or you will be destroyed by each other. (Galatians 5:15)

With all the preaching and teaching going on in the church today, one would think that it would have a tremendous effect on church members and on society as a result. Instead, the continual problems

Chaos

and crises and church splits point to a serious lack of sanctification in the ranks. The preaching, in other words, didn't address the Problem. For example, people love to hear sermons about God's love for them, and how God has plans to bless them – the "positive," uplifting approach to ministry. But they prefer to ignore the sin in their hearts. They don't want to hear negative messages like that. Then when their sin comes out (and it will – God has a way of revealing what is in us – remember Jesus' warning about "by their fruit you will know them"?) we are amazed to see such an ugly side to people's nature.

Why can the cults claim that most of their membership came from mainline churches – Baptist, Methodist, Presbyterian, Lutheran, Catholic? Why is it that so many church people are easy prey to the lies of the Enemy? Why can't people tell truth from falsehood? Because all those years of teaching, from Sunday School through to the sermons, failed to get the truth firmly entrenched in people's hearts and minds.

> Then we will no longer be infants, tossed back and forth by the waves, and blown here and there by every wind of teaching and by the cunning and craftiness of men in their deceitful scheming. (Ephesians 4:14)

Why is it that when a temptation comes along that is too sweet to pass up, or a conflict with other people occurs, that we show our true colors and fail the test of Christianity? I'm not talking about when we put on our "Sunday best," but what we do when nobody is looking – when we are around our wife or children – when a temptation arises – when a crisis happens and we start fighting others for our "fair share" – when someone makes us lose face and our pride is at stake. It's because the ministry of the church failed to change our natures. We end up looking no different from unsanctified unbelievers, to the great shame of the Lord's work.

> They have become filled with every kind of wickedness, evil, greed and depravity. They are full of envy, murder, strife, deceit and malice. They are gossips, slanderers, God-haters, insolent, arrogant and boastful; they invent ways of doing evil;

Chaos

they disobey their parents; they are senseless, faithless, heartless, ruthless. (Romans 1:29-31)

In our culture we've turned our women into prostitutes (even the Muslims refuse to do that!) and insolent feminists, our children into hedonists and materialists, our men into philanderers and effeminate bystanders, our pastors into salesmen and entertainers, our churches into community centers, our services into psychology sessions. We've let our wicked culture reshape the church to 1) take away its effectiveness, and 2) allow for an immoral and self-centered lifestyle. How did all this happen? Why isn't the church waging war against our wicked culture and changing *that*? Because in the last hundred years the ministry of the church has failed miserably to change the hearts of its members. Therefore, there is something wrong with the ministry of today's churches.

- **There is nobody in charge** – I liken our present culture to children running around the house with no adults present. And that includes the churches. Everyone is literally doing "what is right in their own eyes," as if *their* opinion is the only thing that matters.

This relates to the problem that we have, the same problem that the Israelites had, of having an invisible, spiritual God. Though we say he is our King, we in fact don't trouble ourselves to "seek him with all of our hearts" – that's a lot of work to go through. It means praying in the Spirit, cleansing our hearts and minds of sin and worldliness, entering humbly into his presence. So instead of going through the trouble and risking not finding him anyway, we decide for ourselves how to run our lives and our churches.

One writer described it as each of us becoming our own little god. Though we would never admit it – we still claim to be Christians – we almost never consult Christ on anything. The most we will do is ask him to "bless" what we've come up with on our own. We are actually not interested in having Christ rule over us.

The Catholics proclaim that they have a Head of their Church – the Pope. Protestants answer that Jesus is the Head of the Church, not the Pope. Fair enough. But practically speaking, Jesus isn't the head of their churches either – they are. Protestant Christians have replaced the corrupt Papal system with a "figurehead" – a lifeless image that gives a name to their religion but no actual guidance.

How do I know this? Consider the average prayer meeting. Who among the members brings a Bible to the meeting? Almost nobody does, not even the leaders. Even though prayer is supposed to be an encounter with a real God, on his throne, and we are supposed to be seeking his will (made plain in his Word) – even though prayer should be focused on the treasures in Heaven, on the Lord's ways and works, on instructions from the King (all laid out for us to see in his Word) – even though the Bible describes the right way to approach this King in prayer – that doesn't seem to be important to the average church member. They don't want to know what the Bible says about all this. All they want is to use God like Santa Claus, making up their own prayer concerns like a child's Christmas list.

Many of the functions of a church can be characterized in the same way. Instead of checking to see what Jesus wants done, people form their churches around their own goals, their own rules, their own standards. That's easy to see – no two churches are alike. If we were all doing Christ's will, our churches would look alike. But it's amazing how different churches can be, even in the same town. Every one of them claim to be Bible-based, following God's will. Now if that's true, God must have a splintered and contradictory will!

If Jesus showed up in person, if he were really ruling the church, he would make everyone conform to his way of doing things. We wouldn't have the chaos and contradictory behavior that fills our churches now. We can only conclude that someone isn't playing this game by the rules. In fact, Jesus would be making massive changes in many of the churches that you and I are familiar with. How do we know this? The letters in Revelation show Jesus straightening out his wayward churches.

- **Enemies in the ranks** – One of the worst things that can happen to an army, or the country that sends out an army, is to have traitors working inside the ranks. Just when you've got enough problems dealing with the enemy outside, you find the enemy striking at your

Chaos

rear, at your weakest points, cooperating with the outside enemies to bring you down. It just isn't fair. It's also terrifyingly effective, because we didn't expect an attack from one of our own – it can cause a huge amount of damage as well as ruin the army's morale.

When we joined the church we never thought about enemies within the walls of the fellowship. Yes, we read the story of Judas in the Bible, but that was an extraordinary event and Jesus always had the problem well in hand. When it comes to those who profess to believe in Christ, we take them at their word and trust them. We take it for granted that we're all working from the same page.

Then when the moment is ripe, when we are at our weakest or the opportunity for their gain presents itself, the enemy strikes us and we are in shock.

> Even my close friend, whom I trusted, he who shared my bread, has lifted up his heel against me. (Psalm 41:9)

For some of us who love peace, it takes quite a while until we are forced to admit that there are enemies even within the church. It grieves us to think that those for whom we labored and prayed over for their spiritual well-being would stab us in the back and prove treacherous. We lay awake at night wondering – did we fail them? What went wrong? Why would God allow pain and suffering at the hands of the very people who claim to love God and his people? As Paul did, we weep over the ruin of Jerusalem.

> I know that after I leave, savage wolves will come in among you and will not spare the flock. Even from your own number men will arise and distort the truth in order to draw away disciples after them. So be on your guard! Remember that for three years I never stopped warning each of you night and day with tears. (Acts 20:29-31)

> For, as I have often told you before and now say again even with tears, many live as enemies of the cross of Christ. Their destiny is destruction, their god is their stomach, and their

glory is in their shame. Their mind is on earthly things.
(Philippians 3:18-19)

There is a criminal element in the church, as well as in the world. We should have expected that – since we all came in from the world with the hope (at least the confession!) that Jesus would save us from our sins. But some have no intention of reforming. The church for them, unfortunately, is a new opportunity for crime. It is rarely stealing and murder and rape (though, to our shame, there is some of that in the church too). It usually consists of ravaging the flock and politicking.

But mark this: There will be terrible times in the last days. People will be lovers of themselves, lovers of money, boastful, proud, abusive, disobedient to their parents, ungrateful, unholy, without love, unforgiving, slanderous, without self-control, brutal, not lovers of the good, treacherous, rash, conceited, lovers of pleasure rather than lovers of God – having a form of godliness but denying its power. Have nothing to do with them.
(2 Timothy 3:1-5)

As in society in general, there will always be criminals in the church. But unlike society, in the church there seems to be little or no method in dealing with the criminals. When people act up like this in the church and threaten the well-being of the flock, leaders as well as members take either one of two approaches: overlook their sins and deal with them with "Christian love," or start an all-out battle. Neither approach will solve the problem. Society doesn't deal with criminals in these ways, and neither should we.

Jesus told us there would be wolves among the sheep. So did Paul and the other Apostles, as we've seen already.

> Watch out for false prophets. They come to you in sheep's clothing, but inwardly they are ferocious wolves. (Matthew 7:15)

> I am sending you out like sheep among wolves. Therefore be as shrewd as snakes and as innocent as doves. Be on your guard against men. (Matthew 10:16-17)

Chaos

Our first problem is to overcome our reluctance to identify any church member as a wolf – after all, they all sound so pious and well-meaning! It usually takes a thorough beating (perhaps several!) at their hands before a person is willing to admit there is something seriously wrong about their "confession."

The second problem is what to do with them. If we let them run free, they're going to hurt someone – or perhaps they already have. What you have to do to a wolf is to identify it, isolate it, and either chase it away or shoot it. There is no reconciliation with a wolf – that's absurd. You must deal with it summarily before it tears up more of the flock.

But that's precisely what most churches are not doing these days – dealing with wolves in the way that Christ told us to. There are churches who are trying to love the wolves, and there are those who are trying to fight them in their own way; but few churches know how to bring the Lord's principles into play here.

The result is church splits, factions and divisions, hard-feelings, politicking and plotting, confusion – all sorts of pain and grief that come from spiritual criminals having a field day among ignorant sheep.

These signs of chaos – divisions among brethren, contradictory interpretations of the Bible, prevailing sins, no-one in charge, enemies in the ranks – this is a pretty dismal state of affairs. It's interesting that things haven't changed at all over the span of history. We have the same chaotic situation that the Israelites had in their day. That's why David's solutions are so applicable to our problems; that's why Jesus, the Son of David, is determined to do for us what his father David had done for Israel.

We are ripe for a change. But the change has to come from a different source from the ones we've been using. As Israel found out, the king they needed was not one of their own number – though Saul was a head taller than the rest and a stout warrior, that doesn't make a

Chaos

good leader in God's Kingdom. The answer lies in the least conspicuous member of Jesse's family, in the One whom everyone despises. That King knows the mind of God and is determined to carry out God's plans for his Kingdom on earth.

David's Plan

David inherited a mess from King Saul. Under Saul's leadership, Israel fell to her lowest point since some of the disastrous days of the Judges. For centuries, the Israelites had been used to doing whatever they thought was right, without any one person leading the people back to the Law to see what God wanted from them.

> In those days Israel had no king; everyone did as he saw fit. (Judges 21:25)

When Saul was king, Israel had hopes that for once the people would be drawn into a single nation under one head, and they would be able to defeat their enemies and prosper for a change. And at first it seemed that this would happen: Saul won victories over the Philistines. But it wasn't long before Saul showed the true nature of his heart. He began to disobey the Lord's commands and do things his own way. For example, when the prophet Samuel passed on the Lord's command to put every living creature in the Amalekite camp to death, Saul evidently thought that this was an unnecessary waste – so he saved the livestock, and even spared the life of the Amalekite king. When Samuel confronted Saul about not carrying out the Lord's orders, Saul made the excuse that –

> The soldiers brought them from the Amalekites; they spared the best of the sheep and cattle to sacrifice to the LORD your God, but we totally destroyed the rest. (1 Samuel 15:15)

But God isn't interested in our opinions; when he gives us a command to carry out, he expects strict obedience:

> Does the LORD delight in burnt offerings and sacrifices as much as in obeying the voice of the LORD? To obey is better than sacrifice, and to heed is better than the fat of rams. For rebellion is like the sin of

David's Plan

divination, and arrogance like the evil of idolatry. (1 Samuel 15:22-23)

Obviously Saul wasn't going to work out as the king over God's people. The Lord needs someone for the job who will be careful about the Law of Moses, someone who is filled with the Spirit and knows the mind of God, someone who is primarily interested in God's glory and not his own.

So the Lord sent Samuel out to find a replacement, which he found in the shepherd boy David, the eighth son of Jesse. At the time not even his own family – not even the prophet Samuel himself! – thought that this young boy would measure up to the exacting requirements of this position. But the Lord saw something important in David:

> The LORD does not look at the things man looks at. Man looks at the outward appearance, but the LORD looks at the heart. (1 Samuel 16:7)

David, the Lord could see, was "a man after his own heart" (1 Samuel 13:14) who would work to build God's Kingdom, not his own, over the Lord's people.

When David took over as King (you can read about the ceremony in 2 Samuel 5:1-5) he immediately set about working on five critical areas:

- **First, he established a capital city.** The Jebusites, one of the Canaanite tribes who had remained unconquered from Joshua's day, held the fortified hilltop called Jerusalem and dared David to conquer them. They underestimated him. He quickly took it from them and made it his official residence. The story is in 2 Samuel 5:6-10.

    The king needed a capital in a central location for his realm. Up until this time, even in Saul's day, the center of government was wherever the judge or king happened to live – and that changed frequently. The Israelites from

David's Plan

Dan to Beersheba had no one place to bring their problems or concerns to.

David, however, made his kingdom much easier to manage by setting up his throne in Jerusalem. His subjects brought him tribute there, came there for his judgments, and gathered there for the religious festivals. He himself sat on the throne in Jerusalem and sent out his officers from there over the entire nation to carry out his commands. In fact, the city of Jerusalem became identified with the King – it was known as the "holy" city because of it being the seat of the King and the place where God also lived in the Temple.

Setting up Jerusalem as the capital was probably the single most important factor in bringing stability to the nation. Up until this time Israel was just a collection of confused, warring tribes who couldn't pull themselves together to work on anything. But now in one stroke David had turned Israel into a nation in her own right with a king to be reckoned with – with the resources of a nation behind him, both for war and for peace.

- **<u>Second, David finally crushed the enemies of Israel.</u>** For too long the Israelites had been persecuted, harassed and defeated by her pagan neighbors. The book of Judges is a graphic example of her history: because she hadn't exterminated all the Canaanites living in the land, Israel repeatedly suffered at their hands. The Lord would raise up judges to save them from their oppressors, but in a short time the Israelites would go back to worshiping the false gods of their neighbors, and God would punish them with wars and persecution.

At first it seemed that King Saul was going to break the cycle of war and oppression – he did win a few victories over their enemies in the beginning – but when he fell into sin and rebellion himself the Lord again

David's Plan

allowed the Israelites to suffer defeat, especially at the hands of the Philistines.

When David ascended the throne, the time had come to put this issue to rest – permanently. As you can see in 2 Samuel 5, he promptly went to battle against the Philistines and the Moabites and defeated them. What he did to the Moabites shows us how determined he was to settle the issue for good: he put to death two thirds of the men of the nation, in a harsh way! That act alone no doubt impressed the Israelites that they finally had a leader who could deal summarily with the enemy – their foreign policy problems were over.

- **Third, he led the people back to God.** Another problem in Israel was that the pure worship that Moses laid down to them in the Law was almost a thing of the past. Several stories in Judges show us that the people of God had seemingly forgotten how to worship the Lord – false priests, altars to foreign gods, immorality, no justice. The ark traveled around the countryside – it was at Bethel, or at Shiloh, or carried into battle with the army. The religion of the Lord God of Israel seemed to be of little importance to the people. Even the priests – for example, Eli's sons – treated the service of the Lord as an opportunity for personal gain.

It was time to bring the Israelites back to their God. In 2 Samuel 6 we read of David bringing the ark from the house of Abinadab into the city of Jerusalem. After the little problem about Uzzah touching it without authority (and getting put to death for his trouble!) David and the people entered Jerusalem and set up the ark in the tent on Mt. Zion. It was a magnificent ceremony – dancing, singing, worship, food and drink – and it was purposely designed to impress the people with how central the Lord and his worship were to the nation. Whatever the other nations might do, Israel must come together around her God in praise and worship, obeying his Law, offering the stated sacrifices for sin and atonement. David made the principle of centering around God a requirement in his new Kingdom.

The important thing to grasp is that David had to step in and restore the worship of the Lord, because being the head of state he had the authority as well as the responsibility to set an example of what the Israelites must do to please God. The nation will do as the King does; so if David goes back to the Lord, so will his people. And he went on to lead the people again and again to the Lord in worship, as we can see from his many psalms.

- **Fourth, he established a government.** David was only one man. Though he set up Jerusalem as his capital and sat on the throne of Israel, he couldn't go himself and execute the laws of his Kingdom from Dan to Beersheba. He needed a system of government, administrators and officials to carry out his orders.

He made his sons government officials, because he could exert the necessary influence over them to carry out his will. He also had many trusted friends and army comrades whom he made government officials – see the list of some of them in 2 Samuel 8:15-18. These were men who came out to help David when he was an outlaw in the wilderness, hiding from Saul's unjust wrath. Men like these needed to be rewarded for their loyalty.

Of course he wouldn't have picked fools for important government posts. He knew the skills of each man and put them in the places where they would do the most good for the nation. David's goal, remember, was to build up Israel in the fear and knowledge of the Lord. So he's going to make sure that whoever he has in authority over the various aspects of Israel's life will help build that kind of Kingdom.

David's Plan

And the rule of his government was the Law of God. The man who wrote the following lines –

> The Law of the LORD is perfect, reviving the soul. The statutes of the LORD are trustworthy, making wise the simple.
>
> The precepts of the LORD are right, giving joy to the heart. The commands of the LORD are radiant, giving light to the eyes.
>
> The fear of the LORD is pure, enduring forever. The ordinances of the LORD are sure and altogether righteous.
>
> They are more precious than gold, than much pure gold; they are sweeter than honey, than honey from the comb.
>
> By them is your servant warned; in keeping them there is great reward.
>
> Who can discern his errors? Forgive my hidden faults.
>
> Keep your servant also from willful sins; may they not rule over me. Then will I be blameless, innocent of great transgression.
>
> May the words of my mouth and the meditation of my heart be pleasing in your sight, O LORD, my Rock and my Redeemer. (Psalm 19:7-14)

... knew how important it would be to live by God's Law as a nation, not just as an individual. To David it would never be a problem of deciding what was the right or just thing to do, or what justice would consist of – it's all written in God's Word.

- **Fifth, he prepared the plans and materials for the Temple.** Many people think that Solomon, since he built the Temple, must have drawn up the plans for the Temple.

David's Plan

They are mistaken. It was David who drew up those plans. Not only that, he also gathered the materials for the Temple. When he was about to die, he handed over the entire project to his son Solomon – so that all that Solomon had to do was follow the instructions that his father had left him!

David at one point had wanted to build a Temple for the Lord; he felt embarrassed that he had a fine palace to live in while the ark of the Lord was still sitting in the old, original tent that Moses had made hundreds of years ago. But the Lord had someone else in mind as the builder of the Temple. David, the Lord told him, was a man of blood:

> You have shed much blood and have fought many wars. You are not to build a house for my Name, because you have shed much blood on the earth in my sight. (1 Chronicles 22:8)

Not that what David had done was wrong (it was God who gave him victory over his enemies), but that the hands which built this special House must be those of a man of peace.

> But you will have a son who will be a man of peace and rest, and I will give him rest from all his enemies on every side. His name will be Solomon, and I will grant Israel peace and quiet during his reign. He is the one who will build a house for my Name. He will be my son, and I will be his father. And I will establish the throne of his kingdom over Israel forever. (2 Chronicles 22:9-10)

In fact, the name Solomon comes from שלם – *shalom* – which means "peace." The Temple is where God will

David's Plan

dwell among his people in peace – peace between God and man, and between man and man.

But David was going to play an important role in the Temple. The Lord showed him what the Temple must look like, what it must be made of, and even what personnel would work in the Temple and their duties.

> "All this," David said, "I have in writing from the hand of the LORD upon me, and he gave me understanding in all the details of the plan." (1 Chronicles 28:19)

This was appropriate for two reasons: *first*, because David had a special relationship with the Lord and knew the heart of God. God shared his thoughts and plans with David so that he could rule over the Israelites in truth, according to God's Law. So he had an insight into God's ways and works that would result in the kind of Temple that would be acceptable to God.

Second, he was the model king for Israel, and what he did through his realm would be the pattern for all the kings to follow – especially for the Messiah, the Son of David who would sit on David's eternal throne. For this reason the Lord appointed David as the architect of the Temple – for the sake of the work on God's spiritual Temple that Jesus would later build, as the Son of David.

David had his share of problems in life, some of them caused by his own sin and foolishness (for example, his adultery with Bathsheba and cover-up murder of her husband). And the Lord certainly punished David for his sins; not even the King of Israel is above the Law. But even when he sinned, he showed that he had the kind of heart that God wants to see in his servants. For example, Psalm 51 shows us a sinner in the agony of guilt and repentance for his sin. The Lord showed himself a merciful God in how he handled the great sins of David.

David's Plan

The point, however, about David is that he successfully accomplished the five tasks that made Israel a great nation under God. Here was a people who lived by God's Law, who treated each other with justice and righteousness, who trusted in God to take care of them, and who regularly came to God's throne for worship and submitting themselves to his will. What more could God want out of a people than this? They were in a perfect position for him to bless them and lead them – and David got them there when generations of leaders and kings before him failed to do so.

David ruled over Israel for forty years. Being mortal, the time came to turn over the kingdom to his son Solomon and die. But as it says in Ecclesiastes, we can work hard all of our lives and then turn over all that we've worked for to someone who just may mess everything up!

> I hated all the things I had toiled for under the sun, because I must leave them to the one who comes after me. And who knows whether he will be a wise man or a fool? Yet he will have control over all the work into which I have poured my effort and skill under the sun. This too is meaningless. So my heart began to despair over all my toilsome labor under the sun. For a man may do his work with wisdom, knowledge and skill, and then he must leave all he owns to someone who has not worked for it. This too is meaningless and a great misfortune. (Ecclesiastes 2:18-21)

Fortunately Solomon was the wisest man of his age – so he managed to preserve the Kingdom that his father left him. In fact, he made Israel the richest nation in that area, certainly richer than she had ever been or ever will be, and there was peace along all of her borders during his reign. It was Israel's height of glory. But even Solomon had his faults that laid the seeds for future problems.

> As Solomon grew old, his wives turned his heart after other gods, and his heart was not fully devoted to the LORD his God, as the heart of David his father had been. (1 Kings 11:4)

David's Plan

There are two important things to notice in this passage. *First*, David is used as the pattern, the model king of Israel, to whom all his descendants were compared. In other words, David's works were fundamental to the life of Israel and the glory of God. Any king who succeeded him must do as his father David had done in order to get God's approval.

And that's the *second* thing to notice here – all the descendants of David who sat on the throne of Israel *were* compared to their ancestor David. Here even Solomon strayed from the royal program that God expected his kings to follow: whereas David led the people back to God, Solomon began leading them away from God to worship false gods. The result in the long run was disaster and Exile. Do you see? The Scriptures judge a king by whether he followed the five-point plan of David, the model king.

Other kings were judged in the same way:

> He committed all the sins his father had done before him; his heart was not fully devoted to the LORD his God, as the heart of David his forefather had been. (1 Kings 15:3)

> He did what was right in the eyes of the LORD, but not as his father David had done. (2 Kings 14:3)

> He did what was right in the eyes of the LORD, just as his father David had done. (2 Kings 18:3)

The last example was Hezekiah. He was one of the few kings of Judah who got a 100% approval rating from the Lord. And as you can see here, the Lord approved of him because he "did as his father David had done."

The Scriptures also call Jesus the Son of David. For example, these passages use that name when referring to him:

David's Plan

A record of the genealogy of Jesus Christ the son of David, the son of Abraham. (Matthew 1:1)

As Jesus went on from there, two blind men followed him, calling out, "Have mercy on us, Son of David!" (Matthew 9:27)

All the people were astonished and said, "Could this be the Son of David?" (Matthew 12:23)

The crowds that went ahead of him and those that followed shouted, "Hosanna to the Son of David!" (Matthew 21:9)

While the Pharisees were gathered together, Jesus asked them, "What do you think about the Christ? Whose son is he?" "The son of David," they replied. (Matthew 22:41-42)

It was a popular concept – one which these and other passages emphasize – that the Messiah would not only be a descendant of David but would sit on David's throne, ruling over David's kingdom. There's a good reason for that. Many people could claim to be descendants of David; even Joseph, Jesus' so-called "step-father," was a "son of David." But the Messiah would actually rule over the kingdom that was given to David – *and do the same things that his father David had done*. This is the key to understanding the ministry of Christ as he sets up his Kingdom.

The Mission

People attend church for many reasons. Most of those reasons, unfortunately, are things that they made up themselves – to satisfy their conscience, do God a favor, present a favorable community image, for fellowship, family counseling, mate-seeking, tradition's sake, enjoyment of a worship service, entertainment, to voice their opinions, or for political reasons.

So – is anybody interested in why Jesus called us together?

Church is not just another community function, like our jobs or social events or entertainment. But most people would definitely not like the idea of church if they were told its true Mission – to strip us bare, morally and spiritually speaking, in the presence of God and man, start working on this ugly reality of sin in our hearts, and rebuild us into the Kingdom that God wanted in the first place.

> She will give birth to a son, and you are to give him the name Jesus, because *he will save his people from their sins*. (Matthew 1:21)

> Two men went up to the temple to pray, one a Pharisee and the other a tax collector. The Pharisee stood up and prayed about himself: 'God, I thank you that I am not like other men – robbers, evildoers, adulterers – or even like this tax collector. I fast twice a week and give a tenth of all I get.' "But the tax collector stood at a distance. He would not even look up to heaven, but beat his breast and said, 'God, have mercy on me, a sinner.' "I tell you that this man, rather than the other, went home justified before God. For everyone who exalts himself will be humbled, and *he who humbles himself will be exalted*." (Luke 18:10-14)

> But you do not realize that you are wretched, pitiful, poor, blind and naked. I counsel you to buy from me gold refined in the fire, so you can become rich; and white clothes to wear, so

The Mission

you can cover your shameful nakedness; and salve to put on your eyes, so you can see. (Revelation 3:17-18)

I believe that when we dress up in our "Sunday best," we tend to forget about what we are inside, in our hearts. We *look* good, we *feel* good being in church, so we've talked ourselves into believing that we *are* good. We don't like to bring up the ugly truth about what we really are – or what we can be, given the right circumstances. So we shift the emphasis of church to a time of fellowship, enjoyment, fun, productive work – anything but the church's true Mission.

Rebellion against the King

Our root problem is the sin in our hearts. Sin, as the Bible describes it, is rebellion against God's rule over us.

> Everyone who sins breaks the Law; in fact, sin is lawlessness.
> (1 John 3:4)

The nature of sin has been the same since the beginning of time. Eve turned away from God's command. The Israelites turned away from God's rule over them in the time of the Judges. And in our day, it hardly ever enters our minds, when we get up in the morning, to find out what God's will for us might be today – our primary concern is what *we* want to do. It doesn't seem to concern most of us in the least that God has an agenda; our own attitudes and opinions and feelings are all that matter to us.

I can understand why the unbelievers feel this way, but in the church such an attitude is inexcusable. When we became Christians – if we truly became Christians! – we confessed that "Jesus is Lord." (Romans 10:9) Does the name "Lord" not mean anything in today's church? Have our modern democratic attitudes destroyed the old image of a Lord?

What a shame that God's people, who call themselves by his Name, are open to this charge of rebellion against the King! Yet the Scriptures teach us that many in the church do not have a submissive spirit about them. The English Standard Version translates this characteristic as

The Mission

"insubordinate" – in other words, so-called Christians are *not* under the control and rule of Christ. They have no inclination to follow his orders.

> For there are many who are insubordinate, empty talkers and deceivers, especially those of the circumcision party. (Titus 1:10)

A Lord – or a king – was the top of the hierarchy. He literally had all power in the kingdom, to the extent that his commands were carried out on the spot, no matter what they were. The lives of all his subjects were in his hands. There was no democracy involved; there was no appeal from his court. Even if he were a good king, any subject who knew what was good for him would approach with fear and trembling, humbly, bowing down at the king's feet, begging and pleading his case before the throne. We may not like that idea, but any fool who approached the king as we modern Americans would – despising his authority and looking him straight in the eyes – would be immediately put to death. Various stories in the Bible contain illustrations of this.

Jesus Christ the King demands no less homage – he is surrounded with more glory and awe than any mortal king. If I were to give you a reasoned and logical argument why you should come to him humbly with your mouth shut, ready to do *his* will, you might resent my remarks – a cold argument has hardly ever convinced willful and rebellious hearts. So let me show you some examples of how people in the Bible approached the Christ.

> Then one of the synagogue rulers, named Jairus, came there. Seeing Jesus, he fell at his feet and pleaded earnestly with him. (Mark 5:22-23)

> When a woman who had lived a sinful life in that town learned that Jesus was eating at the Pharisee's house, she brought an alabaster jar of perfume, and as she stood behind him at his feet weeping, she began to wet his feet with her tears. Then she wiped them with her hair, kissed them and poured perfume on them. (Luke 7:37-38)

The Mission

Therefore God exalted him to the highest place and gave him the name that is above every name, that at the name of Jesus every knee should bow, in Heaven and on earth and under the earth, and every tongue confess that Jesus Christ is Lord, to the glory of God the Father. (Philippians 2:9-11)

When I saw him, I fell at his feet as though dead. (Revelation 1:17)

And when he had taken it, the four living creatures and the twenty-four elders fell down before the Lamb. (Revelation 5:8)

In fact, the Greek word προσκυνέω behind our English word "worship" means "worship; fall down and worship, kneel, bow low, fall at another's feet." We Americans rarely do that. Muslims bow down to their god, Hindus to their gods, but we can barely bow our heads a little when we "worship" Jesus. It's ironic that even when we sing lyrics like "we fall down before you" – we don't, and we're not going to.

Our attitude runs deeper than our attitude during worship, however. Humility is not just for those times when we want something from the King. If he has issued a set of commands that he wants us to work on, can we really say that we serve the King if we ignore them all? Here are some of his commands:

- Get rid of your sins – all of them.
- Love God with all your heart and mind and strength.
- Train in righteousness.
- Help him build his Kingdom.
- Give him glory in everything.
- Identify, and fight, the Enemy.
- Love your neighbor at least as much as you love yourself.

You must understand that these are not just for when you have a little time to spare for "religion." As far as he is concerned, he expects

The Mission

you to work on these things even to the exclusion of your other daily activities. Notice how he commended Mary for putting aside kitchen duty for the privilege of sitting at his feet and learning from him.

> As Jesus and his disciples were on their way, he came to a village where a woman named Martha opened her home to him. She had a sister called Mary, who sat at the Lord's feet listening to what he said. But Martha was distracted by all the preparations that had to be made. She came to him and asked, "Lord, don't you care that my sister has left me to do the work by myself? Tell her to help me!" "Martha, Martha," the Lord answered, "you are worried and upset about many things, but only one thing is needed. Mary has chosen what is better, and it will not be taken away from her." (Luke 10:38-42)

Though some might complain that we are being unreasonable here – that we simply can't turn our whole day over to pursuing spiritual matters – let's put it in perspective. The truth is that the average Christian spends almost no time in spiritual matters. If you spend ten minutes a day reading your Bible, and five minutes praying – a total of 15 minutes doing "devotions" – that means (out of 1440 minutes in a day) you are giving about 1% of your life to him! That may impress you, but it doesn't impress the King who signed you up for his service.

Lawbreakers

Most people think that they will survive the ordeal of Judgment Day. They know that they've done wrong, that they have broken some of the Commandments, that they didn't do good when they should have. But they also think that they *have* done a lot of good in their lives too. Surely, if God is just, he will weigh the good against the bad and base his judgment on that. Aren't a lot of us good, decent people?

Another variation on this theme is this: "All I have to do is live a good life, and I'll get into Heaven." And that may mean anything from minding one's own business, getting a good job and raising a family, helping out at church bazaars, being patriotic, giving to charities, or who knows what else.

The Mission

In order to judge man fairly, however, God needs a standard to go by. Fortunately he doesn't have to rely on man's laws to provide the standard of what is right and wrong. God has already told us the standard he's going to use on Judgment Day. It's his Law.

You can find the Law in the first five books of the Bible – Genesis, Exodus, Leviticus, Numbers, and Deuteronomy. God first gave this Law to Israel as a precious gift: they alone learned what it would take to please God.

> He has revealed his Word to Jacob, his laws and decrees to Israel. He has done this for no other nation; they do not know his laws. (Psalm 147:19-20)

While the rest of the world wondered how to please God (they never did figure it out), and how to take care of this matter of their sin, the Israelites *knew* how. All they had to do was follow the Law to the letter. And if they did, God would consider them to be *righteous* – which is another word for *good*.

> And if we are careful to obey *all this Law* before the LORD our God, as he has commanded us, that will be our righteousness. (Deuteronomy 6:25)

There are 613 separate commands in the Law of God. For some reason there are many people who think that the Law consists of only the Ten Commandments. Actually the list of Ten is a summary of the other 603 commandments, and the "two greatest commandments" that Jesus refers to in Matthew 22:35-40 are a summary of the Ten.

The point is that God expected his people to follow them *all* – not just a few here and there. They were not free to pick and choose which commands they would follow. Someone who followed all the commands and yet broke a single law would be judged a *law-breaker* and duly punished:

> If you really keep the royal law found in Scripture, "Love your neighbor as yourself," you are doing right.

The Mission

But if you show favoritism, you sin and are convicted by the law as lawbreakers. For whoever keeps the whole Law and yet stumbles at just one point is guilty of breaking all of it. For he who said, "Do not commit adultery," also said, "Do not murder." If you do not commit adultery but do commit murder, you have become a lawbreaker. (James 2:8-11)

The reason this is true about the Law is because they are all tied together. You can't obey just one law! For example, if you want to obey the law of "you shall not murder," that means you also have to do the opposite – you must "love your neighbor as yourself." And love means, according to the Law, a number of things: paying fair wages, laws about interest on debts, helping your neighbor out in his distress, taking care of widows and orphans, how to handle business dealings, dealing with proselytes to the faith, employee relationships, laws about someone's lost property, the laws about tithing, and so on. And don't forget what you must do if you ever break one of the laws: then it would be necessary to bring any of several sacrifices to the priest to get forgiven of your sin, and perhaps having to do something to become ceremonially clean again. In other words, there are *many* laws that spell out what it means to do good to your neighbor – not just one. The Lord didn't leave it up to us to decide what "doing good" might mean.

Plus, there are two ways to keep – or break – the Law. There is the sin of **commission**, in which you do something that the Law forbids. But there is also the sin of **omission**, in which you fail to do something that the Law expects of you. Many people are counting on the fact that they didn't deliberately break one of the Lord's laws; but what they ought to be worried about – in fact, what the conscience of a sensitive person does in fact wonder about – is whatever they might not have done that needed doing. *That* side of the Law will be a surprise for many on Judgment Day.

So when someone says, "all I have to do is live a good life," I wonder if they realize what they're saying. What do they think "good" means? According to God, "good" means living according to *all* the commands of the Law of God! At least that's what is going to cross *his* mind on Judgment Day when these people claim, before his throne, that they lived a "good life."

> Be perfect, therefore, as your Heavenly Father is perfect. (Matthew 5:48)

> Now a man came up to Jesus and asked, "Teacher, what good thing must I do to get eternal life?" "Why do you ask me about what is good?" Jesus replied. "There is only One who is good. If you want to enter life, obey the commandments." "Which ones?" the man inquired. Jesus replied, "'Do not murder, do not commit adultery, do not steal, do not give false testimony, honor your father and mother,' and 'love your neighbor as yourself.'" "All these I have kept," the young man said. "What do I still lack?" (Matthew 19:16-20)

There's an additional problem with the Law. Not only are we expected to follow all of it, the Lord intended that it be obeyed *from the heart*. What good is it if we keep the Law on the outside – with right *actions* – when in our hearts we break the Law continuously with *thoughts and attitudes* of sin? Jesus put his finger on the problem when he taught the true depth of the intent of the Law:

> You have heard that it was said to the people long ago, 'Do not murder, and anyone who murders will be subject to judgment.' But I tell you that anyone who is angry with his brother will be subject to judgment. Again, anyone who says to his brother, 'Raca,' is answerable to the Sanhedrin. But anyone who says, 'You fool!' will be in danger of the fire of hell. (Matthew 5:21-22)

That's going to be a surprise on Judgment Day! When people find out that God intends to condemn sinners for their *thoughts* – that what they felt in their hearts is just as bad a crime, in his eyes, as what criminals did in their actions – the terror of that day will finally settle in.

The Mission

Some people are aware already of the far-reaching power and expectations of the Law. David, who always wanted to please God, pleaded with the Lord to look into his heart – the seat of his actions – to see if there was anything wrong there, before it broke out into open sin. He *wanted* God to use the Law to judge his heart.

> Search me, O God, and know my heart; test me and know my anxious thoughts. See if there is any offensive way in me, and lead me in the way everlasting. (Psalm 139:23-24)

This is sort of a preemptive strike against the problem of sin. Fix the heart, and you won't live in sin. Overlook the heart, and you will naturally live in sin – because we do what is in our hearts.

> But the things that come out of the mouth come from the heart, and these make a man 'unclean.' For out of the heart come evil thoughts, murder, adultery, sexual immorality, theft, false testimony, slander. These are what make a man 'unclean'; but eating with unwashed hands does not make him 'unclean.' (Matthew 15:18-20)

Impossibly high standards? On the contrary – God is simply safeguarding Heaven from another moral catastrophe like the one that first happened in the Garden of Eden. Because of one single sin – Adam and Eve eating the fruit of the Tree of the Knowledge of Good and Evil (and notice that the outward sin was born from the thoughts going through her mind) – all of mankind plunged into moral darkness, murder, ignorance, hatred, war, sickness, misery, rebellion and death. That's the power and destructive force of a heart guided by sin! So the Lord has no intention of allowing sin *of any kind* into his Heaven.

Paul describes the scene of Judgment Day, and God judging our hearts with his standard of the Law, like this:

> For it is not those who hear the Law who are righteous in God's sight, but it is those who obey the Law who will be declared righteous. (Indeed, when Gentiles, who do not have the Law, do by nature things

The Mission

required by the Law, they are a law for themselves, even though they do not have the Law, since they show that the requirements of the Law are written on their hearts, their consciences also bearing witness, and their thoughts now accusing, now even defending them.) This will take place on the day when God will judge men's secrets through Jesus Christ, as my gospel declares. (Romans 2:13-16)

As you can see, there's nothing unfair about God bringing out the whole Law to judge our hearts by. We knew all along, down in our consciences, that he would do this.

I hope you begin to see the problem about planning our defense around our good works. We have a few hurdles to jump here that are too high for us:

First, you probably don't even know what most of those 613 commands are! If the Law is God's idea of being good, how can we hope to be good in his eyes if we don't even know the requirements? If we plan to draw God's attention to a few things that we thought that we did right, what are we going to say when he keeps bringing us back to those hundreds of commands he gave us in the Law that we had no idea about, the laws that we violated without ever knowing it?

In a court of law, the judge isn't interested in the defendant's promises that he will change his life and do good from now on. He isn't interested in any stories about what the defendant did right in the past. And he especially isn't impressed with the argument that the defendant didn't know about the law that he broke ("ignorance of the law is no excuse!"). The law demands an accounting for *the crime that was committed*; someone has to pay for breaking the law. So the judge will first determine if the defendant did indeed commit the crime in question. If the person is guilty as charged, the judge is required by law to pass sentence on

The Mission

him as a lawbreaker. It's a very simple transaction. And once the court has determined that you are a lawbreaker, the only thing left to do is to give you your punishment.

In our current court system, many prisoners depend on the fact that the judge isn't all knowing, and there may not be good evidence or eyewitnesses to contradict his claims of innocence. So there's a chance that even a guilty person will be acquitted. But in God's court there is no such hope. God already knows the facts of the case, down to our very thoughts, and we will never fool him.

> Do not be deceived: God cannot be mocked. A man reaps what he sows. The one who sows to please his sinful nature, from that nature will reap destruction; the one who sows to please the Spirit, from the Spirit will reap eternal life. (Galatians 6:7-8)

Plus, the Law that he uses to judge us demands the blood of the lawbreaker. So he's going to make absolutely sure whether you are guilty of breaking any of his laws – otherwise someone could accuse him of being unjust. He is going to probe deeply into your mind and thoughts to see if you are guilty of breaking any of his Law (any of the 613 commands of the Law, that is). He *has* to dig this deep, because first, the Law is the description of a *perfect man*. To pass inspection, to gain access to a perfect Heaven, you have to satisfy *this* Law. And second, it would never do to let someone slip by the Judgment who is a sinner – Heaven won't tolerate the presence of sinners. Are you ready to face that kind of grueling session?

> For the Word of God is living and active. Sharper than any double-edged sword, it penetrates even to dividing soul and spirit,

The Mission

joints and marrow; it judges the thoughts and attitudes of the heart. Nothing in all creation is hidden from God's sight. Everything is uncovered and laid bare before the eyes of him to whom we must give account. (Hebrews 4:12-13)

Second, we are in trouble because the Law of God expects more from us than we can measure up to. The Law is spiritual

> We know that the Law is spiritual; but I am unspiritual, sold as a slave to sin. (Romans 7:14)

We live on two levels: the outward, physical level, and the spiritual level. Our outward actions *might* be acceptable for the most part to *some* of the Law's demands (in other words, we didn't actually commit a physical murder or commit adultery with someone), but our hearts are stained with the thoughts and intentions of sin.

> They are darkened in their understanding and separated from the life of God because of the ignorance that is in them due to the hardening of their hearts. (Ephesians 4:18)

Sin on one level is just as bad as sin on the other level. The Lord can't afford to let a sinner – someone who has sin in the heart, where it all starts anyway – into Heaven, a place of righteousness and holiness. Before you enter into God's presence ready to justify your actions in life, consider whether you want to put your heart under this kind of scrutiny. Jesus warned us many times not to make that mistake! For example, when the rich young ruler came to him to find out how to get to Heaven, Jesus told the man that he had to follow the Law. And when the ruler responded that he *had* been

The Mission

following the Law, all of his life, Jesus proceeded to open up his heart and show him his hard-heartedness against both God and man. This alone disqualified him for Heaven. (See Luke 18:18-30) It was easy for Jesus to do this, because our heart-sin lies just beneath the surface of our outward actions – hard for men to see, but easy for God to see.

Third, anybody who thinks that they're ready to argue their case on Judgment Day is going against all the accumulated wisdom and warnings of the writers and saints of Scripture. Jesus warned us about how terrible that day will be – we stand an excellent chance of dying in our sins.

> I told you that you would die in your sins; if you do not believe that I am the one I claim to be, you will indeed die in your sins. (John 8:24)

Paul and the other apostles warned us that we don't want to appear before God as we are, no matter how good we think we might be. The prophets warned us about the terrors of the Last Day. Everywhere we look in the Bible, we read the message loud and clear: you would be *much better off* trying to find an alternative to what you are planning to do. You do *not* want to try to defend yourself before this God.

Get one good look at God as he really is and you will understand everyone's alarm. He is a terrifyingly holy God, a God of fire and judgment, and he does not tolerate fools.

> Therefore, since we are receiving a kingdom that cannot be shaken, let us be thankful, and so worship God acceptably with reverence and awe, for our "God is a consuming fire." (Hebrews 12:28-29)

The Mission

He doesn't even need our explanation for our actions – he wouldn't even trust us to pass judgment on our own hearts.

> But Jesus would not entrust himself to them, for he knew all men. He did not need man's testimony about man, for he knew what was in a man. (John 2:24-25)

> His eyes are on the ways of men; he sees their every step. There is no dark place, no deep shadow, where evildoers can hide. *God has no need to examine men further*, that they should come before him for judgment. *Without inquiry* he shatters the mighty and sets up others in their place. (Job 34:21-25)

> I care very little if I am judged by you or by any human court; indeed, I do not even judge myself. My conscience is clear, but that does not make me innocent. It is the Lord who judges me. Therefore judge nothing before the appointed time; wait till the Lord comes. He will bring to light what is hidden in darkness and will expose the motives of men's hearts. At that time each will receive his praise from God. (1 Corinthians 4:3-6)

When the saints of the Bible saw God on his throne, they knew right away that they needed to find an alternative to the foolish notion of meeting him face to face without help:

> "But," he said, "you cannot see my face, for no one may see me and live." (Exodus 33:19)

The Mission

> "Woe to me!" I cried. "I am ruined! For I am a man of unclean lips, and I live among a people of unclean lips, and my eyes have seen the King, the LORD Almighty." (Isaiah 6:5)

> When I saw him, I fell at his feet as though dead. (Revelation 1:17)

The first task of the church, then, is to finally solve this problem of sin to God's satisfaction. Otherwise we have no hope of life after this one. We have to get to the very root of our problem; we have to uncover our unacceptable attitude of rebellion and willfulness and lawlessness and present our naked hearts to God, the purifier of souls. We have to open up completely, hiding nothing, desiring nothing short of complete perfection – the perfection of Christ's own nature. We want his pure Spirit reigning completely, uncontested, in our lives. Church is the time for humility, confession, repentance. As one writer put it, if the church is following its Mission, we should come away from the church service humbled and chastened.

We believe and trust in God's love, but the *purpose* of that love is to draw us into his presence to be cleansed thoroughly from our innate wickedness. The love of God simply means that he's not going to blast us in condemnation when we come before him! His purpose is to save us from what is killing us. He wants us back – just as the father took back his Prodigal Son – but the rules are going to change. What a fatal mistake to think that focusing on God's love in church sets aside the need for our thorough salvation! It's time to take hold of this opportunity that God has given us and work on **The Problem**.

Earth-bound

Another characteristic of many "Christians" (we're not going to bother discussing out-and-out unbelievers, since we know where they stand on these issues) is that they have little interest in the next world. Of course they all claim to believe in Heaven, and they claim to want to go there after this life. In other words Heaven, to them, has little or no impact on their lives here and now.

The Mission

Again, the Israelites were the same way. Once they settled into the land of Canaan, they did exactly what God predicted they would do.

> Be careful that you do not forget the LORD your God, failing to observe his commands, his laws and his decrees that I am giving you this day. Otherwise, when you eat and are satisfied, when you build fine houses and settle down, and when your herds and flocks grow large and your silver and gold increase and all you have is multiplied, then your heart will become proud and you will forget the LORD your God, who brought you out of Egypt, out of the land of slavery. (Deuteronomy 8:11-14)

There is sin here too, but mainly it's a matter of ignorance. *We may have been made citizens of Heaven, but we are totally unprepared to go there.* We know almost nothing about Heaven, and if we were suddenly transported there we would feel totally out of place. We hardly know who God is, and we are not yet aware of how unfit we are to live in such a place.

To live with God we must be prepared first. This is the work of Christ's Spirit. To be concise, the Spirit does several things for us.

- **First,** he is the Spirit of Christ – so he fills our hearts to make us one with the Son of God. This is the mystery that Paul talked about. We don't know how he does it, or exactly what happens to us when he indwells us – but we who have been converted know that "Christ lives in me." We now have the mind of Christ, the wisdom of Christ, the power of Christ, the love of Christ. We've been freed from the *power* (though not the presence) of our old master, sin, and we now belong to Christ as a bride given to the bridegroom. If we don't understand or even know much about this special union with Jesus, that only shows how much we have to do to get oriented to our new relationship with God.

- **Second**, the Spirit of course is going to remake us to "conform us to the image of Christ" – he makes us look

The Mission

like Jesus. Not physically, but spiritually. "Righteous" is the key word here. God will not tolerate the least sin in his pure Heaven. And the only form of righteousness that he's interested in is the pure and total righteousness of his son Jesus. Though the believer now has that by a gift – he is *legally* righteous in God's eyes – the reality has to catch up to the legal status. Our relationship to God – the privilege of approaching him in faith and resting on all the inheritance that Jesus bought for us – is in place and operating. But the purpose of that first legal step is to bring us into the spiritual world of powerful resources to finish the job. We now must *become* righteous, down to our very core. This second step is called sanctification, when our natures become like Christ.

- **Third**, the Spirit reveals the spiritual world of God to us and weans us away from this physical world. The world we're in now is doomed; God intends to take it apart and remake it into a spiritual world for us to live in. It makes sense, therefore, to get used to a new way of doing things – a new language, a new house, new inhabitants, new responsibilities, new joys and pleasures. We have to learn God's ways and how to work with him, not against him. If Christ is our bread and our light, we have to begin feeding on him and following him in his light. God himself is going to be our chief delight now, because in him is the reality that will give our spirits the most joy and pleasure.

As you can see, there is a lot of work to do to get us ready to live with God. The problem is that most Christians are almost unaware of this new world, let alone willing to devote much time for preparation to go there. Their hearts are in this world – like Lot's wife. It's difficult if not impossible to get them interested in a world that they can't see and that seems to have little to no impact on their present circumstances. They are much more interested, as Paul tells us, on filling their bellies. (Philippians 3:19)

The Mission

The Spirit's job is to get us ready for this new world. But when God's people resist the Spirit's preparations, it disturbs him. The Bible calls this *grieving the Spirit*.

> And do not grieve the Holy Spirit of God, with whom you were sealed for the day of redemption. (Ephesians 4:30)

When the Spirit knows what we need to do to get ready, and has all the resources at hand to do the job, and gives us ample opportunities to work on this — and then we fight him, resist him, put him off, reject his influence and direction, we can hardly expect God to be pleased with us. He's trying to lead us to life and we are trying to go back to bondage! At some point God may just back away and let us wallow in our worldly filth for a while – in Exile – and wait for us to wake up to the importance of Heaven. *That* isn't going to be pleasant!

Summary

The Mission of the church is twofold:

- **<u>First</u>**, we have to be thoroughly delivered of our sins – our immorality, our waywardness, our ignorance, our willfulness, our rebellion, our lawlessness, our independent attitude. The job of the Christian is to come back to God, humble himself, submit to his rule, and serve him. We have to *change*, from sinner to saint. The ministry of the church *has* to address that need.

- **<u>Second</u>**, we have to start getting used to the new world that Jesus is preparing for us. We have to put our minds on things above, learn God's ways, live in the righteousness of Christ, start frequenting the Temple in Heaven, wean ourselves away from this physical world and start storing up treasures in Heaven, learn to be holy and set apart for God's use.

There's a lot to be done in these two areas. It's surprising that so many people are doing hardly anything to address these key issues and yet they still have hopes of Heaven someday. It will take all the

The Mission

resources of a church's ministry to successfully prepare its members for this kind of life. I know, it's not much fun to focus on your sin when you go to church. It's like finding out that we have cancer, or going through a heart attack. It's not exactly what we were planning to do with our free time! But this problem has been forced upon us, and now we have to deal with it or die. *The Bible's entire message revolves around this issue of what is going to be done about our sin.*

People naturally want the church to address other problems in their lives – family problems, job problems, neighbor problems, financial problems, health problems. But Christians have to understand that these, though important, are *not* the primary Mission of the church. These other issues will be addressed, even some of them solved, *only if people focus on the two main issues of our faith.* If we make real progress on the primary Mission, that will start straightening out other problems along the way. This is the teaching of God's Word.

The Mission

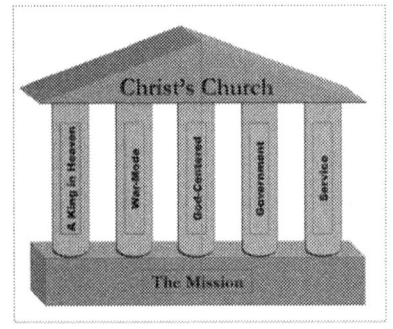

Part Two

A King in Heaven

Location is everything. Businesses understand that when they locate their stores in high-traffic areas. David understood that when he took Jerusalem from the Jebusites and made that his new capital. God understood that when he located his new nation right in the path of the Middle East trade routes and cultural byways. Jesus understood that when he ascended to Heaven after his resurrection.

In order to understand why Jesus located his capital in Heaven, we have to know what the goal of Christianity is. The goal is *not* to make our lives here more secure and comfortable; as we've seen already, the goal is to move on to another world. It's the spiritual world that we are heirs to. Jesus went on ahead of us to prepare a place for us *there*.

> In my Father's house are many rooms; if it were not so, I would have told you. I am going there to prepare a place for you. And if I go and prepare a place for you, I will come back and take you to be with me that you also may be where I am. (John 14:2-3)

The place where Jesus sets up the throne of his Kingdom greatly affects what kind of ministry ought to be going on in a church.

A Spiritual world

The Old Testament has confused a lot of people because of its heavy emphasis on the physical, even though God took great pains to explain it to us. One of the most important aspects of the Bible is how the physical and spiritual levels interact with each other in the timeline of God's recorded works.

A King in Heaven

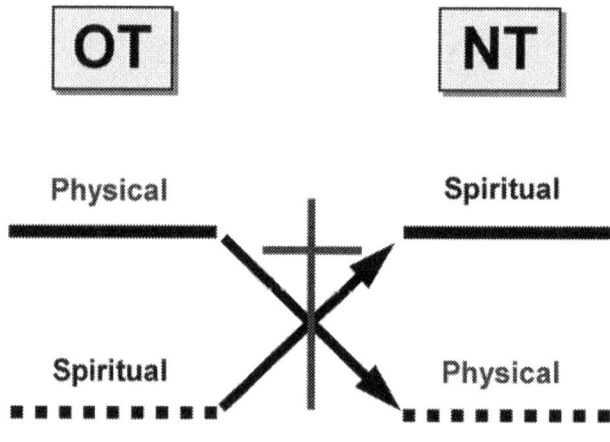

Physical & Spiritual Levels

- In the **Old Testament**, the *physical* level predominates. We see animal sacrifices in a physical Temple. We see the children of Israel settling down in Canaan. We watch David pulling the tribes together and defeating the Moabites and Philistines. Just about everything we read about is something that we can see, feel, or hear with our physical senses.

God did this for a reason. Since the solution to mankind's problems of sin and death is so complex – and since the ultimate solution is a spiritual one which nobody can see – he started out by teaching us the answer on a level that we could easily grasp. It's amazing how much even children can learn if you make your point in the form of stories and pictures.

So to teach us lessons of his spiritual world in terms that we cannot mistake the meaning of, he used stories of his works in the lives of real people in real places. The point is there for anybody to see; a child can understand the story; and if we read and believe what God is saying, we can be saved.

A King in Heaven

Some of the important stories of the Bible include the following:

The Creation of the world
Abel's sacrifice
The Flood
The Covenant with Abraham
The Blessing of Jacob
Deliverance through Joseph
The Exodus
The Promised Land
David and Solomon
The Divided Kingdom
Punishment and Exile
Rebuilding the Temple and the walls of Jerusalem

We miss the point if we think that these events (and many others) were merely physical events that happened to the Jews only. The Bible was written for all of us; the whole Church is the recipient of God's letter. The physical events recorded in the Old Testament describe the same things that happen in God's spiritual world *in all ages*.

Yet we also catch a glimpse of the spiritual just behind the physical, right underneath the surface, if we have the eyes to see and ears to hear. Passages like the following show us that God always did consider the physical level to be temporary and not the ultimate point:

> "The multitude of your sacrifices – what are they to me?" says the LORD. "I have more than enough of burnt offerings, of rams and the fat of fattened animals; I have no pleasure in the blood of bulls and lambs and goats." (Isaiah 1:11)

A King in Heaven

Didn't he tell the Israelites to bring these sacrifices to him at the Temple? Yet here he is claiming that he doesn't want them! The point is that they were hiding behind the animal sacrifice as if that would cleanse their souls, and then going right back into their sin. This is not the way to worship God! The sacrifices were designed to teach us how terrible is the effect of sin. We're supposed to stop our sinning. If anything, the sacrifice would point up the need for something more permanent that would change the heart, so that we wouldn't sin anymore. The sacrifices of the Temple were an embarrassing reminder of the weakness of the system.

Paul also gives us clues that some of the Old Testament saints understood the ultimate point of a spiritual kingdom.

> A man is not a Jew if he is only one outwardly, nor is circumcision merely outward and physical. No, a man is a Jew if he is one inwardly; and circumcision is circumcision of the heart, by the Spirit, not by the written code. Such a man's praise is not from men, but from God. (Romans 2:28-29)

Surprisingly, this idea was first explained in the Old Testament Law!

> The LORD your God will circumcise your hearts and the hearts of your descendants, so that you may love him with all your heart and with all your soul, and live. (Deuteronomy 30:6)

- In the **New Testament**, the *spiritual* level predominates. The situation flip-flops, so to speak. Now instead of a physical Temple, we learn of the Temple in Heaven that we must come to. Now instead of a physical land of Canaan to inherit, we inherit Heaven. David

A King in Heaven

sitting on the throne in Jerusalem turns into the Son of David sitting on his throne beside the Father. The Philistines aren't a problem to us anymore, but our sins and the "spiritual forces of darkness" certainly are.

Of course the situation in the Old Testament was also spiritual, but they were required to learn and work things out through the physical means that God gave them. Only by faith would they realize that a more permanent solution would eventually come to light. Now, however, the veil has been taken away, the time has come; the eternal solution has been revealed to us.

The Gentiles need to learn the lessons of the Old Testament so that they can understand their faith. The Jews need to graduate from their physical system so that they can finally enjoy the reality of God's salvation. Either way, we don't need the physical anymore. It has served its purpose; the lessons are now recorded in the Old Testament for all to learn. Those lessons are a stepping stone, a primer to something better. Why long for the shadow when you can have the real thing? That's why the Apostles urged us to leave the physical behind and, through faith, reach out for the eternal realities.

> The blood of goats and bulls and the ashes of a heifer sprinkled on those who are ceremonially unclean sanctify them so that they are outwardly clean. How much more, then, will the blood of Christ, who through the eternal Spirit offered himself unblemished to God, cleanse our consciences from acts that lead to death, so that we may serve the living God! (Hebrews 9:13-14)

We do have a few minor physical aspects to our religion, however. We gather together in church buildings, we are baptized with water, we eat bread and drink wine at the communion service, we have preachers and teachers who train us with the Word of God. But we understand (or we're supposed to!) that these can't touch the soul as the Holy Spirit can. The reality isn't in the things we use in our religion; those are "vessels" through which God touches us with the treasures from Heaven. We know now that we can pray anywhere, not just in Jerusalem – because the Spirit lifts us up to the Throne of Heaven.

Our list that we used above – the physical items that God used to lead Israel – is still important to us, but now on a spiritual level.

OT – Physical	NT – Spiritual
The Creation of the world	*The New Creation*
Abel's sacrifice	*The sacrifice of Christ*
The Flood	*This world will be destroyed*
The Covenant with Abraham	*The Gospel of Christ*
The Blessing of Jacob	*Treasures in Heaven*
Deliverance through Joseph	*Deliverance through Christ*
The Exodus	*Leaving the world behind*
The Promised Land	*Heaven*
David and Solomon	*King Jesus*
The Divided Kingdom	*Division in the Church*
Punishment and Exile	*Discipline of God's people*
Rebuilding the Temple and the walls of Jerusalem	*Building the Church*

Remember that this list is a short one; there are so many lessons to be learned in the Old Testament and they all have spiritual counterparts in Christ's Kingdom. God's Kingdom used to be on earth, among the Jews, and they first learned what it's like to live with this God. Now the Church is living with him, and they too must learn the same lessons. The difference is that we are in training for living with a spiritual God that we can't see or touch.

The New Testament emphasis

The New Testament never encourages us to turn our faith into a springboard for "health and wealth," as some ministries try to do. Paul knew that there would be some in the church who think a relationship with God means being blessed with the good things of *this* world.

> For, as I have often told you before and now say again even with tears, many live as enemies of the cross of Christ. Their destiny is destruction, their god is their stomach, and their glory is in their shame. Their mind is on earthly things. (Philippians 3:18-19)

Both Jesus and the Apostles directed our attention to the next world, not this one.

- **We are looking forward to spiritual treasures** – *Do not store up for yourselves treasures on earth, where moth and rust destroy, and where thieves break in and steal. But store up for yourselves treasures in Heaven, where moth and rust do not destroy, and where thieves do not break in and steal. For where your treasure is, there your heart will be also.* (Matthew 6:19-21)

    Most Christians wouldn't know what to say if you asked them what those spiritual treasures are. Pearly gates? Streets of gold? The saints in the Bible disdained the wealth of earth; they willingly turned their backs on wealth and riches so that they could gain things that enriched their spirits. To them, a chance to be holy as Jesus is holy drew them to God. The opportunity to see God's glory as he really is was worth more to them than anything earth had to offer. The love of God in Christ, peace in their souls, justice that straightens out the unfathomable mess of history, wisdom to see the purpose and plan of God in Creation – these are treasures worth dying for. And to live forever in the presence of God – the Creator, the Father, the only Good, the source of all good things, the Holy of Holies, the eternal light – is a bliss that all true saints are looking forward to. If they arrived in Heaven and found this world's gold and treasures there, they would be deeply disappointed and confused. They were told to consider such trifles as nothing compared to eternal treasures!

- **We are citizens of Heaven** – *Their mind is on earthly things. But our citizenship is in Heaven.* (Philippians 3:19-20)

    A citizen has both rights and responsibilities. A citizen of Heaven has the right to come before God's throne – even closer, to sit at his right hand as one of his children. We have this right because we are one with Christ, the Son of God. Our union with Jesus brings us into the closest relationship possible with God: living in his love, privy to his deepest counsels, co-regent with him over the Creation.

    Being heirs of Abraham, we have inherited the promises of the Covenant which are found in Christ – eternal life, cleansing from all sin, a spiritual home to live in, a new kingdom to rule over, being part of the family of God, the right of access to God. All this is ours now. Our present life here on earth is only temporary, while we prepare for our eternal home.

    And of course our responsibilities are also those of Christ Jesus, who serves as Priest for the family of God, the Heir who dispenses the riches of the Covenant to God's family, the Holy One who fulfills the Law to God's glory. We have an amazing future ahead of us as we look forward to sitting at God's right hand over the universe.

- **We are aliens here in this world** – *Dear friends, I urge you, as aliens and strangers in the world, to abstain from sinful desires, which war against your soul.* (1 Peter 2:11)

    If anybody wondered what our relationship with this world would be once we became Christians, the NT writers leave no doubt. Pack your bags, you're leaving! You don't belong here. Your stay here will be short, your life from this point will be training for the next world, and your relationships with others temporary. Now even "father and mother" aren't as close to you as your Father in Heaven. It would be a mistake to form close relationships with people who hate your God and do not share in your hopes for eternity. It would be fatal to tie your flesh to temptations and pleasures that will not survive the grave. It's time to say goodbye to all of that.

- **We look forward to our new home** – *Since, then, you have been raised with Christ, set your hearts on things above, where Christ is seated at the right hand of God. Set your minds on things above, not on earthly things.* (Colossians 3:1-2)

    If this world is not our home, if the spiritual world of Heaven is to be our home for eternity, wouldn't it make sense to spend time learning what that world is like? It's important to know that it's a Kingdom, that God rules over it in justice and peace, that its subjects are those whom Jesus described in the Sermon on the Mount (Matthew 5-7). We need to learn the language and customs and even the dress codes of this new home if we want to fit in there (see Matthew 22:12 for an example of someone who didn't!).

There are many other passages that show us how much Jesus and the Apostles did not value this world, looking forward instead to the next one. Jesus had nowhere to lay his head; he denied being a king of this world; he was a man despised and forsaken, a man of sorrows. Paul willingly went through beatings and persecution and privation; he considered his troubles "light and momentary" in comparison to his inheritance in Heaven; he even considered his "blessings" in this world (those things that others put a lot of stock in) as so much dung. James called the poor of this world "blessed" because they were free of the burdens of material riches and open to the joy of spiritual treasures, and he felt it necessary to warn the rich of the dangers of their wealth.

A King in Heaven

The point is that any church that wants to pattern its ministry after the New Testament saints must steer its members to Heaven, not to this world.

Stepping stones to the spiritual

Of course it's going to be difficult to orient yourself to a spiritual world – you can't see it, you are unfamiliar with its ways, and it's hard to appreciate an inheritance that you can't really enjoy until after you die. The Israelites struggled with the same difficulty, trying to live under the rule of a spiritual God.

But just as God gave David to the Israelites – a King who would make the reign of God real to them – in the same way he has given us a King who will make the reign of God real to us. But it's time to graduate to spiritual matters; the physical was good for teaching us the right lessons, but it doesn't save the soul. So Jesus ascended to his throne in Heaven and is now at work ruling over us, his subjects, using the *spiritual* principles that we learned in the Old Testament – principles that will hold true for the rest of eternity.

To make our connection with the spiritual world of Christ possible, Jesus has given us two stepping stones that will help us reach from this world to the next. He told the woman at the well about them.

> Yet a time is coming and has now come when the true worshipers will worship the Father in **Spirit** and **truth**, for they are the kind of worshipers the Father seeks. God is spirit, and his worshipers must worship in **Spirit** and in **truth**. (John 4:23-24)

• **<u>The Truth</u>** – The first stepping stone to Heaven is the Bible. The Bible is the Word of God, the truth that Jesus refers to here. "Your Word is truth." (John 17:17)

"Truth" means the way God sees things. We have our own opinions and viewpoints, but never can we see any problem or situation the same way that the Creator sees it.

A King in Heaven

When you know all the angles and you're not missing anything important, that puts you in a position to make a right judgment about it and take the appropriate action. It's when we don't have all the information that we end up doing something wrong or missing the point.

Imagine always being able to see everything around you the way God sees it! You would miss nothing, you would never be surprised, you would know exactly what to do and when to do it. Men dream of wisdom and insight on that level.

But that's what God has given us in his Word. It's just that he isn't very interested in what *we* want to know about – making money, becoming more powerful, getting more pleasure, building up security. So the Bible doesn't discuss those issues much, and therefore most people aren't very interested in the Bible.

What the Bible does reveal to us is the world of God. It goes to great lengths showing you the spiritual inheritance you have in Christ, the spiritual treasures that you can lay up in Heaven. It shows you the glory and majesty of God, his ways and works, his powerful Names and how to use them. It shows you the spiritual forces of darkness in this world and the many traps you can fall into that will put your soul in jeopardy if you aren't careful.

People don't always see these things in the Bible, but that's because they are too perverse to read and understand plain writing. It's there on every page. What they want to see – what their spiritual blinders will only let them see – is what they can get out of God to serve their own lusts and desires.

> In them is fulfilled the prophecy of Isaiah: "You will be ever hearing but never understanding; you will be ever seeing but never perceiving. For this people's heart has become calloused; they hardly hear with their ears, and they have closed their eyes. Otherwise they might see with their eyes, hear with their ears,

A King in Heaven

understand with their hearts and turn, and I would heal them." (Matthew 13:14-15)

God gave them a spirit of stupor, eyes so that they could not see and ears so that they could not hear, to this very day. (Romans 11:8)

What does the Bible tell us of *this* world? Mainly that it's a dangerous place, that everything "under the sun" isn't worth the effort that people put into it. It tells us that your life here will be painful, frustrating, unfulfilling. You will have enemies on every side.

It encourages us, instead, to look to God's spiritual world. There is life; there is where our hope is. For those who have eyes to see, the entire Bible paints a glorious picture of the Promised Land, and what it will be like to live with God there. The entire Bible is actually the story of our journey to life in Heaven with God.

- **The Spirit** – Jesus told us that when he ascended his throne in Heaven he would immediately pour out his Spirit on his followers – which we read about in Acts 2.

People seem to be really confused about the work of the Spirit – probably because certain groups have lifted a few verses out of context and turned the work of the Spirit into a highly subjective, ecstatic experience. But really the work of the Spirit can be divided into two areas.

First, the Spirit reveals the world of God to us. The things that we read about in the Bible are just so many stories from the past until the Spirit makes them real to us. There is a fundamental difference between Christianity and all other religions: we know our God is real because we've seen him. Other religions can only talk about a god they've heard about from their traditions; we have seen the living Christ. That is, in fact, what it means to be a Christian – through faith we have seen the invisible and we know it is real.

A King in Heaven

> By faith he left Egypt, not fearing the king's anger; he persevered because *he saw him who is invisible*. (Hebrews 11:27)

Second, the Spirit enables us to use and enjoy those spiritual realities we see in God's Word. The Spirit of Christ literally lifts us up into the halls of Heaven, empowers us to take hold of the spiritual treasures there, and fills us with the power of Christ to live *before God*.

> Taste and see that the LORD is good; blessed is the man who takes refuge in him. (Psalm 34:8)

> But you have come to Mount Zion, to the Heavenly Jerusalem, the city of the living God. You have come to thousands upon thousands of angels in joyful assembly, to the church of the firstborn, whose names are written in Heaven. You have come to God, the judge of all men, to the spirits of righteous men made perfect, to Jesus the mediator of a new covenant, and to the sprinkled blood that speaks a better word than the blood of Abel. (Hebrews 12:22-24)

By means of these two stepping stones – the Word and the Spirit – we can reach Jesus in Heaven and he will rule over us. *It is vitally important that any local church be firmly established on these two realities.* These are the life of the Church.

> The Spirit gives life; the flesh counts for nothing. The words I have spoken to you are spirit and they are life. (John 6:63)

A Christian needs revelation from Jesus, that continuous vision of his real home and love. The deeper the picture, the clearer the picture, the sharper and more powerful will be his faith. There is no such thing as too much Bible study! The Bible has to be fully expounded (particularly the Old Testament, since in many ways it is the best description of life with God in his Kingdom) in order to give a full

A King in Heaven

picture of God and Heaven, the hope of the Christian – because this is what his faith feeds on. The most serious problem that any church can have is the lack of understanding on the part of the teachers – that they themselves fail to dig deeper into the Word, and so pass on a shallow understanding of the Bible to the sheep. The Old Testament suffers the most here because people understand so little about it.

And to keep it from becoming a sheer intellectual exercise, the church has to grasp the reality of this truth – through prayer and worship through the power of the Spirit. Prayer seeks the reality of God with passion and persistence. It seeks answers from a God who listens and hears and blesses his people with treasures from Heaven according to the Word. It cleanses the heart and soul, and positions a believer in the path of holiness and righteousness, to make the road to Heaven clear of obstacles so that answers will come. It's a powerful way to set God's people up for the realities of Heaven.

Worship also enables us to touch God by offering up praises to him who is deserving of praise. It focuses on God and his works and nature. It humbles the believer before this God on his throne, empties his own will, and prepares him for God's rule over him. And it makes him open and willing to hear the Word of the Lord through the teaching of the church.

Why do Christians miss this?

People like physical comforts and security. For all their talk about loving God and serving him, you will lose their attention if they are hungry, sick, frustrated, opposed, confused, or tempted. Our five senses are tuned to this world, not the next; we understand perfectly how valuable a dollar is, but we can't see how spiritual treasures can help us.

Religion is easy when all you ask of a person is to show up Sunday morning (maybe Sunday evening too, if there's not a ball game on TV). In church, people sing hymns with gusto, recite the general principles of Christianity with zeal, and pat each other on the back for their Christian "witness." But if religion requires hours and hours of study and meditation in the Bible – well, they don't have time for that. If it requires severe soul-searching to root out the little as well as big sins in their hearts – well, they feel they've made enough progress already and don't need any more improvement. If it requires looking across the aisle and finding out what their neighbor really needs from them – well, they gave their offering already, so don't ask any more of them.

There are at least three kinds of people who miss entirely the spiritual aspect of Christianity:

- **The Pharisees** – The villains of the Gospels, they earned their sinister reputation fairly. They placed all their hope in keeping the Law of God by their own efforts. They thought they could do it; they talked themselves into thinking that they were good people who lived in the perfection of the Law. They couldn't see the open door to Heaven in Jesus.

    Some Pharisees who were with him heard him say this and asked, "What? Are we blind too?" Jesus said, "If you were blind, you would not be guilty of sin; but now that you claim you can see, your guilt remains." (John 9:40-41)

    God rewarded their obstinacy with a spiritual blindness that closed their eyes to the life that is in Jesus. Therefore their entire lives, their whole worldview, focused on *this* world. To this day the religion of the Jews centers on the physical world that they live in – almost nothing of the next world. The ecstasy of Paul in the first chapter of Ephesians as he surveys the spiritual treasures in Christ is a foreign and repulsive concept to the Jew.

    I am concerned that many present-day Christians are also focused on this world instead of the next. Like the Jews, they have been blinded to God's spiritual world by legalism and by their obstinate self-righteousness that will prompt the Lord to close the doors of Heaven to them. Their "faith" has turned into a smug, worldly religion without Christ.

A King in Heaven

- **<u>Those seeking bread</u>** – When Jesus did a miracle and fed thousands of people out in the fields, a lot of people were understandably impressed. Here is a good thing, they thought – we need to stay close to this man who can take care of us so easily.

They missed the point. Yes, Jesus can take care of our physical needs. But those miracles were only pointers to deeper needs that we have – and there is where Jesus' interest lies. He has not come to keep feeding us bread, something we can do for ourselves with a little work and responsibility. He has come to give us spiritual food, something we can't do for ourselves.

> For even when we were with you, we gave you this rule: "If a man will not work, he shall not eat." (2 Thessalonians 3:10)

> I tell you the truth, you are looking for me, not because you saw miraculous signs but because you ate the loaves and had your fill. Do not work for food that spoils, but for food that endures to eternal life, which the Son of Man will give you. On him God the Father has placed his seal of approval. (John 9:26-27)

But too many people are only interested in earthly pleasures that satisfy their physical lusts and desires. They turn Christianity into an earthly religion too – their prayers center on God giving them food, clothing, shelter, family, possessions. Their testimony is of how faithfully God provided all these physical things. The blessings they hope for are a long and prosperous life, and freedom from sickness and want. They almost never think about their souls.

> So do not worry, saying, 'What shall we eat?' or 'What shall we drink?' or 'What shall we wear?' For the pagans run after all these things, and your Heavenly Father knows that you need them. But seek first his

A King in Heaven

kingdom and his righteousness, and all these things will be given to you as well. (Matthew 6:31-33)

> The ground of a certain rich man produced a good crop. He thought to himself, 'What shall I do? I have no place to store my crops.' Then he said, 'This is what I'll do. I will tear down my barns and build bigger ones, and there I will store all my grain and my goods. And I'll say to myself, "You have plenty of good things laid up for many years. Take life easy; eat, drink and be merry."' But God said to him, 'You fool! This very night your life will be demanded from you. Then who will get what you have prepared for yourself?' This is how it will be with anyone who stores up things for himself but is not rich toward God. (Luke 12:16-21)

It's disappointing to hear Christians talk about Christ's faithfulness only in terms of physical, earthly blessings. They miss the point of his ministry.

- **The wicked** – Those who are determined to live in sin are, of course, shut out from the presence of God.

> So I tell you this, and insist on it in the Lord, that you must no longer live as the Gentiles do, in the futility of their thinking. They are darkened in their understanding and separated from the life of God because of the ignorance that is in them due to the hardening of their hearts. Having lost all sensitivity, they have given themselves over to sensuality so as to indulge in every kind of impurity, with a continual lust for more. (Ephesians 4:17-19)

Unfortunately this kind of person is in the church as well. Both Jesus and the Apostles warned us about this. It may take a little time before they show their colors, but eventually their innate wickedness will come to the surface and everyone will see plainly that they had no interest in the spiritual kingdom of God. The only thing they wanted was the freedom and opportunity to rebel, steer others astray, receive glory for themselves, destroy the work of the Lord, and hurt the flock with their greed and politicking. But they have absolutely no awareness of God's spiritual world. Why did they bother to come to church in the first place? Because as we shall see, the church is like an unguarded field of helpless sheep to fleece.

The Churches in Revelation

When Jesus examined the churches in Asia Minor he found some that were spiritually minded and some that definitely were not. Probably the most striking example was the church in Laodicea.

> You say, 'I am rich; I have acquired wealth and do not need a thing.' But you do not realize that you are wretched, pitiful, poor, blind and naked. I counsel you to buy from me gold refined in the fire, so you can become rich; and white clothes to wear, so you can cover your shameful nakedness; and salve to put on your eyes, so you can see. (Revelation 3:17-18)

This church was obviously engrossed with power, wealth, prestige, reputation – it looks like the beginning stages of what the church turned into during the Middle Ages. Church was a source of great wealth and political power for many opportunists in the culture.

But in Jesus' eyes it was poverty-stricken. It may have had all the marks of worldly wealth, but it had none of the treasures of Heaven. Evidently they didn't think it worth their while to focus on the next world. Any poor sheep who wandered into their assembly hall looking for good news of a spiritual inheritance went away hungry, perhaps despised by the rich and powerful there. The church was in sad shape – in fact, it was a shame and disgrace to God's Kingdom.

I'm sure there have been a lot of "Christians" who have read this account in Revelation and yet it never dawned on them that they might be in the same sad shape. Jesus rebuked the Laodiceans, yet we don't have any record of whether they took his rebuke to heart. We do have history's record that most churches in the next two thousand years were

A King in Heaven

Laodicean in nature – and therefore spiritually dead. So there were many people who didn't heed Jesus' counsel.

Would a sin-sick soul wandering into *your* assembly hear about the new home in Heaven, holiness and righteousness being the standards of Heaven, peace with God and wisdom from Christ, life and light in the Spirit? Or would he hear sermons on "asserting our dominion" here in this world, the blessings of wealth, how to be a successful businessman or parent, or pulling oneself up by one's own bootstraps and living right?

Spiritual treasures are found all through the Bible; that's the purpose of God's entire Word. But it takes wisdom and insight to see that. A short-sighted view of the Bible will use only a few favorite passages here and there to teach an emasculated version of the Gospel in Christ; there's no spiritual fullness and satisfaction in a superficial ministry. And it takes wisdom to see that the Kingdom that the Bible teaches is of Heaven, not of earth.

Summary

Jesus left this world and ascended into Heaven to establish his capital city *there*. That fact ought to alert us to the need to shift our focus from this world to the next. What we need as followers of Christ are the treasures and resources of Heaven, not of earth. He rules from Heaven through his *Word* – which is a description of God's spiritual world – and through his *Spirit* – who makes that spiritual world real to us. Our Mission is to put this earth behind us and prepare for life in God's new Kingdom in Heaven. The time has come for Christ's churches to change their focus from earth to Heaven.

War Mode

Most people are like sheep. They don't like to fight. And in a relatively peaceful society like ours, there's no need to fight – just go to work, raise the family, take vacations, and enjoy life.

But as the saying goes, sometimes the fight comes to you, and you can't avoid it.

Fighting in the church is the last thing we want to do. Church fellowship should be a matter of love, peace, building each other up in the faith, forbearance, tolerance, and long-suffering. If people are fighting each other, that's usually a sign that there's something seriously wrong.

> What causes fights and quarrels among you? Don't they come from your desires that battle within you? You want something but don't get it. You kill and covet, but you cannot have what you want. You quarrel and fight. You do not have, because you do not ask God. (James 4:1-2)

On the other hand, what are the victims to do when someone comes into the church and terrorizes the flock? Are they to simply roll over and let the wolves have a feast? Isn't someone responsible to chase away the wolves and protect the flock? Jesus distinguished himself from false shepherds over this very point.

> The hired hand is not the shepherd who owns the sheep. So when he sees the wolf coming, he abandons the sheep and runs away. Then the wolf attacks the flock and scatters it. The man runs away because he is a hired hand and cares nothing for the sheep. (John 10:12-13)

Somebody has to know how to wage war against the enemy! Leaders in particular are responsible for the well-being of the flock. If they shy away from a confrontation with the enemy because "they don't like to fight," they will be branded cowards – and God particularly despises cowards.

> But the *cowardly*, the unbelieving, the vile, the murderers, the sexually immoral, those who practice magic arts, the idolaters and all liars – their place will be in the fiery lake of burning sulfur. This is the second death. (Revelation 21:8)

In order to protect the borders of his new Kingdom, David went to war. Jesus also goes to war to protect his church.

The Enemy

In every war there are two parties: the one who started the trouble, and the one who is defending himself. Usually the one who starts the war is the culprit, and though he might justify his actions in his own mind, it's not so easy to convince his neighbors of his good intentions in light of all the trouble he is causing. His victim occupies the moral high ground – everyone understands that he has a right to defend himself against aggression.

It may come as a surprise to you, but you are *surrounded* by enemies. Like it or not, you are in the middle of a war. And your enemies are bringing the conflict right to your doorstep.

The first step in any conflict is to identify the enemy. We have to know, first, who exactly is trying to destroy us, and second, we have to be willing to call them the enemy. The first step is crucial in any church, since people are just too willing to fight the wrong enemy – usually each other! The second step comes hard for those who love peace. If we don't admit that we are at war, and take steps to deal with the enemy, we will most certainly be destroyed.

So, first things first. Just who are our enemies in the church?

- **The World** – *Do not love the world or anything in the world. If anyone loves the world, the love of the Father is*

War Mode

not in him. For everything in the world – the cravings of sinful man, the lust of his eyes and the boasting of what he has and does – comes not from the Father but from the world. (1 John 2:15-16)

There are two meanings to the word "world" in the Bible. God made the world, in the beginning, and it was beautiful; his Creation was "very good" in his eyes. That's why John 3:16 says that he so loves the world. But here in 1 John the word "world" means what man, and his partner Satan, has turned God's world into – a drunken orgy, so to speak. We've recreated God's perfect paradise into a playground for our lusts, passions, murders, greed, robberies, insurrection, etc. The new world "system," we could call it. It is a world full of temptation, where the opportunities for immorality abound. It's like a circus where people wander from sideshow to sideshow, tasting this forbidden sweet, trying that immoral practice – all set up for our pleasure.

And if we think that we leave the world behind us at the church door, we are foolish. Each of us has been programmed by the world system since the day we were born. We church-goers still think the way the world taught us to think, and our whole being still responds strongly to the world's ways and temptations. Each of us, as the saying goes, brings a lot of baggage with us into the church – baggage that interferes with our Mission.

The world works in ways that God despises. It loves numbers, power, winning, destruction and slaughter, oppression, wealth, influence, reputation, politicking, lies and deceit, hatred, living for pleasure. This is the way it solves its problems and satisfies its lusts. People who live like this have nothing to do with God, nor do they understand him.

- **The Flesh** – *Those who live according to the sinful nature* [Greek σάρξ, "flesh"] *have their minds set on what that*

War Mode

nature desires; but those who live in accordance with the Spirit have their minds set on what the Spirit desires. The mind of sinful man is death, but the mind controlled by the Spirit is life and peace; the sinful mind is hostile to God. It does not submit to God's Law, nor can it do so. Those controlled by the sinful nature cannot please God. (Romans 8:5-8)

As if we needed more trouble, our very natures are to blame for the trouble we get into. We can't just blame the world – or our parents, or our genetic makeup, or the devil – we sin because we *want* to. As Eve discovered in the Garden, the temptation appeals to our desires; and so, using our desires as the standard, we take action on the temptation.

Animals were made with instinct – God wired their brains to dictate their behavior. It's not a matter of choice for them. Man, on the other hand, was made with the same physical desires that the animals have *but with a will to control them*. This will must follow God's Law, not the dictates of desire. But ever since the fall of man, we have all been led by our physical needs and lusts – they dictate most of our actions in life. We live for pleasure; "if it feels good, do it!" The urge to take hold of the temptation is so strong because we have been feeding our flesh all the pleasures we can get hold of. That makes the urge to get more pleasure all that much stronger after every feeding. So now we have a raging monster on our hands – our lusts – that we can't control anymore. It's our own fault.

> For the sinful nature desires what is contrary to the Spirit, and the Spirit what is contrary to the sinful nature. They are in conflict with each other, so that you do not do what you want. (Galatians 5:17)
>
> The acts of the sinful nature are obvious: sexual immorality, impurity and debauchery; idolatry and

witchcraft; hatred, discord, jealousy, fits of rage, selfish ambition, dissensions, factions and envy; drunkenness, orgies, and the like. I warn you, as I did before, that those who live like this will not inherit the kingdom of God. (Galatians 5:19-21)

They are darkened in their understanding and separated from the life of God because of the ignorance that is in them due to the hardening of their hearts. Having lost all sensitivity, they have given themselves over to sensuality so as to indulge in every kind of impurity, with a continual lust for more. (Ephesians 4:18-19)

Again, even when we start going to church, we are a bundle of inflammable desires just waiting for the temptation that will ignite us to sin. That's why it's so easy even for church members to fall into the sins of the flesh – we've been feeding this flesh all our lives, and a few sermons on "love" aren't going to change our natures. We need strong cures to address the problem directly.

- **The Devil** – *You belong to your father, the devil, and you want to carry out your father's desire. He was a murderer from the beginning, not holding to the truth, for there is no truth in him. When he lies, he speaks his native language, for he is a liar and the father of lies.* (John 8:44)

The plot thickens, as most stories do, with the introduction of the arch-villain. Without going into the early history of the devil, Satan was there at the beginning with Adam and Eve to help the temptation process along. He has access to the powers and riches of the world, and he knows how to present its temptations to our fleshly desires to awaken the response he's looking for – rebellion and treason against God. Not that we can blame him for our sins; we are still guilty and fully responsible. But it sure doesn't help matters that we have such a formidable and ruthless opponent who is determined to destroy us – and he knows all too well how to do that.

The principle danger with the devil is that he is almost always disguised. We don't usually realize that he is working in our lives. If we did, it would make things so much easier – to be able to see the enemy is half the battle. But he can use anything and anybody. He covers himself with plausible excuses and even a guise of religion that deceive us.

The devil is a master of lies and deceit. Satan's main method is to lie to us, to deceive us and get us to believe anything other than the truth of God. His statement to Eve was mostly the truth, with a little twist in it that deviated from the truth. He deliberately denied that God would put them to death: "You will not surely die."

Satan wanted to achieve two things in the Garden of Eden: *first*, to get Eve to doubt the Word of God. Always, the devil's aim is to steer us away from the Truth of God to believe anything else, it doesn't matter what. Only the Word of God has life in it; so Satan will lead sinners to believe and trust in anything but the Bible – or, if he can't take us away from that, he will pervert our understanding of the Bible and have us believe that. *Second*, he wanted to deceive Eve about the real outcome of the matter, that she was in no danger if she ate of the fruit.

There's a phrase in the New Testament that reveals a hidden but dangerous aspect of sin:

> But encourage one another daily, as long as it is called Today, so that none of you may be hardened by *sin's deceitfulness*. (Hebrews 3:13)

Sin is deceptive; it misleads us by not showing us the entire truth. Like a worm dangling on a hook, or a piece of cheese tempting a mouse onto a trap, the temptation to sin leads us into a hidden but open door to death.

The deceit, the lie that the devil was using here, is common to all temptations: ***you can do this and get away with it!*** Nobody will know. Nothing bad will happen. That's the lie that often makes the difference with us and coaxes us into the forbidden area. Between making the sin attractive, and hiding the dark threat behind the scenes, we fools reach out and take what is offered with the vain hope that it will be good – a rose without thorns. A little thought beforehand about the way God made his world (that is, everything that is hidden will eventually be made plain) would undeceive us very quickly, but sinners typically rush in without thought – or, what is worse, doubting that God's threat is real. And so we fall prey to the trap.

Did we leave the devil at the door when we came into church? Most certainly not! He can sneak in through anybody who isn't aware of his schemes.

> If you forgive anyone, I also forgive him. And what I have forgiven – if there was anything to forgive – I have forgiven in the sight of Christ for your sake, in order that Satan might not outwit us. For we are not unaware of his schemes. (2 Corinthians 2:10-11)

> Jesus turned and said to Peter, "Get behind me, Satan! You are a stumbling block to me; you do not have in mind the things of God, but the things of men." (Matthew 16:23)

Satan is present in the church as well as in the world, and his work is, unfortunately, all too effective.

These, then are the enemies that we Christians are up against. You may have been surprised that this list didn't include your neighbor, the one you're not speaking to for various reasons. We would like God to side with us in our battles against our enemies. But usually *our* battles are over the wrong reasons; we should be praying for those who oppose us so that God would give them a change of heart. Our real enemies are out to destroy our souls and our relationship to God.

> For our struggle is not against flesh and blood, but against the rulers, against the authorities, against the powers of this dark world and against the spiritual forces of evil in the heavenly realms. (Ephesians 6:12)

War is a serious matter

Too many churches are not in war mode – at least not with the right enemies. For some reason they think that Jesus has already taken care of everything for them, and Christianity now is simply a matter of enjoying the good life. It's as if we are in party mode instead; "celebrating," I believe, is the operative word here. And what exactly are we celebrating? The fact that we have Jesus. But why did Jesus come to us? To deliver us from our sins. (Matthew 1:21) To destroy the works of the devil. (1 John 3:8) To condemn the world. (John 16:8) In other words, we're in the middle of a war! It would make more sense to postpone the celebrations until we've won a few victories. "The end of a matter is better than its beginning." (Ecclesiastes 7:8)

It's as if a man were told he has acute appendicitis, but the doctor assured him that surgery will take care of it. The man goes home and celebrates the doctor's assurances, and then winds up dead the next morning from a ruptured appendix. At what point do we put the celebrations on hold and actually apply the remedy to our sin? At what point do we take up arms and fight the "good fight of faith" against the enemy?

Sin is destroying the world. I don't think we need to belabor that point here. It is a deadly cancer that must be eliminated if we have any hope for life. What makes it even more deadly is that our enemies have been wearing us down, little by little, over years. For most of our lives we didn't know it was happening, and we're still not aware that we've sustained as much damage as the Bible says. It's hard to fight this problem; we've been immersed in it for so long that we're used to it.

War Mode

The point is that sin didn't leave your body when you walked through the church doors. Remember the Mission of the church: it's a spiritual hospital, and you are there to be fixed, cured, cleansed. Just as the priests had to cleanse their bodies and clothes as they entered the Temple, so you must cleanse yourself of your sin as you come before God. If you don't address this problem of yours in a decisive manner, sin will destroy you too – in spite of the fact that you go to church every Sunday. Only Christ's fountain can cleanse us from our sin.

Sin has saturated your soul to the extent that everything you do and think is tainted with it. The world has programmed you so well that you naturally think in the ways of the world, not according to God's ways. Satan has deceived you over and over in your life, to the point that often you would be hard put to know truth from error.

I know that most people don't believe this about themselves, but time will tell. For those who accept the Bible's judgment of them, the Lord will deliver them from their sin and train them in his ways. But for those who refuse to see the danger they are in – there is only trouble ahead. We can be there when it happens and tell them, "I told you so" – but that's small consolation for the loss of another soul.

Not ready for war

A country at peace is a perfect target for a vicious enemy. The standing army is too small to respond to a serious threat. The citizens are working on their prosperity, their children's future, the pleasant pursuits of life. They are not aware of, nor are they much concerned about, enemies on their borders.

Right now most churches are like this. In spite of the fact that we are surrounded by enemies, even enemies within our ranks, our churches are sleeping.

> ***Christians can't seem to identify the true enemy*** – Many don't like to fight, so they don't even want to face the fact that we are at war. Many are fighting the wrong enemy. It grieves me to see brothers and sisters in the faith, both contending for

War Mode

the Gospel of Christ, at each other's throats. Church is not a war with fellow Christians, nor is it a matter of competition. Our war should be a determined and intelligent attack against those enemies that are trying to separate us from God.

There's no discipline for war – War requires a lot of training, memorization, studying, practice. Yet there is almost none of this in today's churches. Sermons are like shotgun pellets – lots of points, scattering all over the place, almost nothing hitting the target. Nobody is required to train at anything or learn anything; there's no home work to do, no tests to take, there's no way of knowing whether anything is getting through. Ministries almost compete with each other at making church easier, less demanding, and more "fun" for the entire family.

There are few resources available – In war we need materiel, manpower, transportation, machines, supplies. An impoverished army will lose every time. But in church we have almost nothing available to fight with – few trained personnel, a serious lack of communication, little to no spiritual treasures or firepower at hand, no fortresses, few if any weapons either offensive or defensive. Hardly anybody even thinks in terms of logistics, though it's one of the most vital aspects of battle.

No defense against savage attacks – The gates of the church are so broken down that, as the enemies of Nehemiah once claimed, "if even a fox climbed up on it, he would break down their wall of stones!" Opportunists, politicians, the sexually immoral, liars and cheats, thieves, gossips and others seem to have free rein to ruin churches. These ravagers of the flock do whatever they want in the name of God, in the house of God, while members and leaders stand on the side either oblivious to the problem or wringing their hands, not knowing what to do or powerless to do anything.

We've forgotten our Mission – The Mission of the church is to fix sinners, to prepare sinful man to live with a holy God.

War Mode

That message is so rare in today's churches that it's become painfully obvious we have laid down our swords and given up the fight. We have been convinced by the enemy to surrender, and now he is ravaging us. We aren't changing into Christ's image.

This is why the church is no longer making an impact on our society. This is why the ministry of the church is failing to change people's hearts and lives. We are no longer in war mode; so we are a defeated nation. We are a disgrace to the Lord's honor.

There's a humbling and embarrassing reason for our defeat. When the Israelites kept losing battles against their enemies, they had to do some serious soul-searching. Almost always they lost battles because they had wandered away from God; they turned to false gods, forgot about the true God and his worship, and as a result fell into immorality. Those who worship false gods always turn out that way.

> After that whole generation had been gathered to their fathers, another generation grew up, who knew neither the LORD nor what he had done for Israel. Then the Israelites did evil in the eyes of the LORD and served the Baals. They forsook the LORD, the God of their fathers, who had brought them out of Egypt. They followed and worshiped various gods of the peoples around them. They provoked the LORD to anger because they forsook him and served Baal and the Ashtoreths. In his anger against Israel the LORD handed them over to raiders who plundered them. He sold them to their enemies all around, whom they were no longer able to resist. Whenever Israel went out to fight, the hand of the LORD was against them to defeat them, just as he had sworn to them. They were in great distress. (Judges 2:10-15)

If God is for us, Paul once taught us, who can be against us? (Romans 8:31) But if we're living in defeat before the enemy, it's not because God's arm is too short to save us. The problem is with ourselves. If we lose contact with God, we're putting ourselves at the "tender mercies" of our enemies and we will suffer all by ourselves. When we need God to protect us and fight for us, and *he's not there*,

War Mode

that means we have another, more important matter to attend to. It's time to humble ourselves before his throne and repent of our sin against him. Then God will give us victories over our enemies. In other words, *remember the Mission.* For a powerful example of this attitude of repentance, see both Daniel and Nehemiah when they went to the Lord for deliverance from their enemies. Their first step was to repent of their sins. (Nehemiah 1; Daniel 9)

God is a warrior

If man and the devil had not rebelled against God, we would have found him to be all love and peace. There would have been no war between us. But our sin has brought God to the point of wrath – an attribute of God that we little understand or appreciate. *He hates sin with all his being.* Sin, to God, is so unacceptable that it must be destroyed – as well as those who persist in it. The wicked are going to see an aspect of God that nobody can imagine.

God responds to his enemies in wrath. I know you can't imagine the destructive force of an atomic bomb; it's beyond human comprehension. But that's a speck, a mote of dust, compared to the wrath of God against sinners. Who in their right mind would risk such an encounter? But what is even more unimaginable is not the powerful impact of God's wrath against us, but that he even feels like that against us. The fury of God against the wicked is not wrong, nor out of place, nor is it something that will go away after a while. He truly, to the bottom of his being, hates the wicked; he always will. (Psalm 11:5)

If we don't understand this, it's because we have no idea what we've done to him. And I'm not sure it does much good to explain it to people, because they look at God as they do some earthly judge who dispassionately hands out a sentence for a crime and can conceivably be talked into being lenient toward the guilty. God does neither. We may get a faint idea of God's feelings if we compare it to slapping a man in the face, or messing with his wife. There will be no mercy.

> Jealousy arouses a husband's fury, and he will show no mercy when he takes revenge. He will not accept any

compensation; he will refuse the bribe, however great it is. (Proverbs 6:34-35)

God is so good, he is so fulfilling, he is so glorious and majestic, he deserves so much honor and praise, his Kingdom is so perfectly run, that when some fool of a sinner rejects God for any reason the entire universe reacts in shock. This sinner is like a cancer cell running loose in a healthy body. He is a blight in the pristine Creation, a cloud of darkness in the Kingdom of Light. He is an offense and a shame in an otherwise perfect world.

> They are clouds without rain, blown along by the wind; autumn trees, without fruit and uprooted – twice dead. They are wild waves of the sea, foaming up their shame; wandering stars, for whom blackest darkness has been reserved forever. (Jude 12-13)

Here is where we see a side of God that we didn't expect. He goes on the war path. He will not allow this blight, this spot of filth and rebellion, in his Kingdom. His aim is all-out war. And don't let yourself sympathize with the wicked, as if you would blame God for being so ruthless and wholesale in their destruction. If you could see them as God does, you would be just as revolted over their true nature. They are just as repulsive to God as a rotting corpse – because they're *dead*, separated from the life of God.

The entire Bible records the wars of God, Old and New Testaments. He thrust Adam and Eve out of the Garden and denied them access to the Tree of Life. He wiped out the population of the entire planet in the great Flood (except for Noah and his family). He scattered the nations at the Tower of Babel to prevent them from forming together against him. He armed and led his people Israel in innumerable battles against their enemies – through Moses, Joshua, Gideon, David, Hezekiah, Nehemiah and others. Jesus led the charge against the Pharisees; he also came specifically to destroy the works of the devil. Paul battled forces of darkness armed with God's armor. And at the end of time, the great Warrior, the King of kings and Lord of lords, will ride for the last time against his enemies and finally destroy them all.

War Mode

I saw Heaven standing open and there before me was a white horse, whose rider is called Faithful and True. With justice he judges and makes war. His eyes are like blazing fire, and on his head are many crowns. He has a name written on him that no one knows but he himself. He is dressed in a robe dipped in blood, and his name is the Word of God. The armies of Heaven were following him, riding on white horses and dressed in fine linen, white and clean. Out of his mouth comes a sharp sword with which to strike down the nations. "He will rule them with an iron scepter." He treads the winepress of the fury of the wrath of God Almighty. On his robe and on his thigh he has this name written: KING OF KINGS AND LORD OF LORDS. (Revelation 19:11-16)

I know it's the current practice for churches to focus on the love of God, and celebrating, and lots of touchy-feely issues that satisfy the effeminate. But study the Bible for a while with war in mind. If you can understand what God is doing, it's not surprising to learn that he wants us to train for battle and enlist in the war that he's waging.

Praise be to the LORD my Rock, who trains my hands for war, my fingers for battle. (Psalm 144:1)

Finally, be strong in the Lord and in his mighty power. Put on the full armor of God so that you can take your stand against the devil's schemes. For our struggle is not against flesh and blood, but against the rulers, against the authorities, against the powers of this dark world and against the spiritual forces of evil in the heavenly realms. Therefore put on the full armor of God, so that when the day of evil comes, you may be able to stand your ground, and after you have done everything, to stand. (Ephesians 6:10-13)

Therefore, since Christ suffered in his body, arm yourselves also with the same attitude, because he who has suffered in his body is done with sin. (1 Peter 4:1)

War Mode

God provides us with offensive and defensive weapons and tactics. He gives us firepower from Heaven. He provides weapons against our enemies that they can't stand up to.

> For though we live in the world, we do not wage war as the world does. The weapons we fight with are not the weapons of the world. On the contrary, they have divine power to demolish strongholds. (2 Corinthians 10:3-4)

Yet God retains the right to lead the army. He knows we can't fight these battles on our own and win. Besides, our enemies are actually in rebellion against God – they hate us only because we represent the God they hate. This is God's battle, not ours. We follow, we train, we fight in his Name, but the victory is his and the glory is his.

> All those gathered here will know that it is not by sword or spear that the LORD saves; for the battle is the LORD's, and he will give all of you into our hands. (1 Samuel 17:47)

> The world cannot hate you, but it hates me because I testify that what it does is evil. (John 7:7)

Rescue the perishing

Some churches do understand that they are in a war. They see the souls of the world dying under the weight of their sins, and they understand their Mission to go out and rescue these people and try to bring them into the safe fold of the church. Hymns encourage this, preachers hit the streets with the message, and revivals are designed to do this very thing.

Unfortunately the fight stops once they get inside the church. It seems as if we think that, once they confess to be Christians and they are safe inside the fold, we can change the subject and assume they don't need any more changing. They've done the right thing to come to church, and we are sure they will continue to do the right things in church.

War Mode

That doesn't square with reality. Church members are still sinners, as you can tell if you follow them home or to the job site. Like the seed that fell on rocky ground, they are excited about Christianity for a while and then lose their zeal once life goes back to the same old round of problems and frustrations. And since sermons in churches like this continually circle around the "come up front and get saved" theme, they have no way to grow out of their old natures. In fact, we too often tend to ignore the fact that sin that is still in us, as if our Sunday clothes puts it out of mind.

The war against sin, against the world and the flesh and the devil doesn't stop at the front door of the church. The fight is only beginning. People are still hurting, and the ministry has to dig down to the root cause of that hurt – the willful, rebellious attitude that so saturates our minds and hearts against the will of God. Conversion simply changes our attitude. It makes us *willing* to address the problem of our inherent sin and come to be cleansed from it.

The preaching and teaching of the Word is critical here. Those teaching the flock must be absolutely faithful to the plain meaning and intent of the passage. Keeping in mind our Mission, the pastor has to "step on toes" – not to beat the sheep and make them fear him, but to faithfully make plain Jesus' judgment of them and offer them a way of escape from what is so hurting them. You know a pastor is being faithful to the truth when he will even preach about his own sins! When he agonizes over a passage both before and after the teaching session, examining his own heart to see if he needs this balm too – that's a pastor worth having. But a teacher who avoids what condemns his own heart, who won't tell people the truth for fear they will reject him or leave the church – that's what Jesus means about a "hired hand." He's not doing what the Chief Shepherd sent him to do. He will be found doubly guilty on Judgment Day.

The battle against our enemies must be ruthless. Church is not a matter of what little we can do and still be called Christians! Our goal is perfection, nothing less. If people get the idea that Christianity is only for Sunday mornings, that they can live as the world does the rest of the week – they will despise the Lord's truth and Kingdom. Our faith must be reflected in how we talk, how we think, how we use our time, our attitude toward everything and everybody, who we relate to and who we don't relate to, what we support with our time and money. The world should be amazed at how seriously we take our religion. Our relationship to God should take first priority; all other things take second place. And keep in mind how dangerous it is to fraternize with the enemy – as the saying goes, bad company corrupts good manners. Be separate from the world; come out from among them if you want to get anywhere with God. (2 Corinthians 6:17) It is time to cut our ties with the enemy.

It requires a lot of discipline on everyone's part to stick to the Mission of the church. That's another way you can tell that the entire church is in war mode – when the entire church throws itself into this battle against our enemies, and helps each member in his or her individual struggle. This is where we need real help, so let's design the ministry around this need. Why do prayer sessions, for example, *always* center around sick people? They need prayer, to be sure, but the Lord's will is that we all be cured of our *spiritual* sickness! We need to be real about baring the needs of our souls, and compassionate toward one another in our spiritual needs.

> Therefore confess your sins to each other and pray for each other so that you may be healed. The prayer of a righteous man is powerful and effective. (James 5:15)

Let no one be left behind in this spiritual struggle against our enemies.

Enemies in the church

Our three enemies are, unfortunately, working hard even in our churches. But we have to be able to correctly identify the enemy. You will almost always find someone you don't like, or can't get along with, in the church you attend. That doesn't make him or her an enemy in God's eyes! Just keep in mind that there are plenty of people who think the same about you!

War Mode

Sinners attend church – and there is the open door for our enemies to attack. But the attack comes in different forms, according to the opportunity presented. There are four kinds of sinners in the church.

- *Unbelievers* – We don't always know whether a church attendee, or even a member, is a true believer. Either they haven't revealed their hearts to us yet, or their confession of faith in Christ (which is, unfortunately, untrue) misled us.

  The strategy here is to keep them from infecting the flock, once their status is known. If they are there seeking help, there are all sorts of ways to bring the resources of the church and its members to bear on the need. But if they are there to make trouble, it won't be long till they tire of being in a holy atmosphere – they will leave on their own eventually. The church has to make it plain to them that sin is unacceptable behavior; it's time to *change*.

- *The Clueless* – The average Christian is a sinner, whether he or she knows it or not. They still have a lot of baggage from the world when they come into the church. Rarely has this ever been pointed out to them, so they aren't really aware of how much they need to change.

  Dealing with sin in the congregation requires the wisdom of Christ. The teachers and leaders of the church must always address sin as sin – unacceptable to God, cleansed by the blood of Christ. But once that is said, it's best to let the Spirit apply the truth to an individual's heart, as only he can do. It's nothing but bad news for the well-being of the church for a pastor to beat the sheep over general sins.

  On the other hand, if a member is committing what is known as "open, gross sins" – for example, those listed in 1 Corinthians 6:9-10 – then the leaders must go to the offending parties and start the process of Matthew 18. And it is most important to follow through on whatever is needed to address that sin, even to the point of showing someone to the door who refuses to honor the Lord's code of morality.

- ***Wrong-headed*** – These people are usually crusaders – well-meaning, but ignorance guides them into passionate displays of zeal and yet they're still wrong. They can cause confusion and bickering and party spirit and a lot of damage if not dealt with properly.

    Peter, in spite of his calling and training to be the Lord's disciple, was once wrong-headed about the Mission of Christ. Jesus had to rebuke him sharply as being an unwitting dupe in the devil's hands. If Jesus had done what Peter wanted, none of us would be saved! What Peter was pleading for was the very plan of the devil. When a church member is being used like this, "they must be silenced, because they are ruining whole households by teaching things they ought not to teach." (Titus 1:11) But the goal, of course, is to deal with them with the hope that they will realize their mistake and come back to the Lord's wisdom and ways.

- ***Wolves*** – These are the hypocrites, the really sinister members of the church. Like the Pharisees, they think only of themselves, they are not spiritually alive, they care nothing about the grace of God in Christ, yet they pass themselves off as righteous people. They are up to no good; the flock will suffer as long as they are around. Your duty as a leader is to chase them away or shoot them.

    It takes a great deal of discernment to know when you're up against a wolf. You don't want to accuse a well-meaning but wrong-headed member of being a Pharisee. But once you've identified your man, *you must isolate him and destroy his influence in the group.* You don't reconcile with wolves; such an idea is absurd and dangerous to the rest of the flock. We are after peace here – peace for the sheep. So get rid of the troublemaker.

War Mode

> Warn a divisive person once, and then warn him a second time. After that, have nothing to do with him. You may be sure that such a man is warped and sinful; he is self-condemned. (Titus 3:10-11)

The Churches in Revelation

Jesus was in war mode when he dictated the letters to the churches in Asia Minor. He ruthlessly targeted his enemies, and made it plain to the church members that he approved of their attitude of war toward their enemies.

He identified his enemies by name. "Wicked men" – "false apostles" – "synagogue of Satan" – "Jezebel." These are not words of love and reconciliation! He had harsh things to say about the enemies of the churches; he wanted the churches to deal with them immediately and decisively, before they poisoned the believers. For example, when the churches tested those who came to them with false doctrine and rejected those men, he praised them.

Jesus planned to come himself, if necessary, and fight against his enemies. "These are the words of him who has the sharp, double-edged sword." (Revelation 2:12) "Otherwise, I will soon come to you and fight against them with the sword of my mouth." (Revelation 2:16)

It's obvious from these letters that Jesus has zero tolerance toward anybody who would hurt his flock. He stands firm against all sin and temptation to sin. He hates Satan and his ways. He insists that the churches come out of the world and be holy, cleansing their garments stained with the sins of the world. Every letter is filled with his zeal against his enemies. And he requires his churches to be filled with the same zeal.

Summary

In this world the church is still the *militant* church – it is not the time for laying down our weapons. Our enemies are continually on the offensive to try to destroy us. The world and its temptations and ways

War Mode

of doing things, our own flesh and its weakness toward those temptations, and the devil with his deceitful way of leading us into trouble and disaster – these are the enemies that we have to contend with. Christ has equipped us with the weapons and the wisdom to destroy them. But we have to put ourselves in war mode. It's time for the church to train and get disciplined to fight.

God-Centered Ministry

The Bible is about God. If you stop reading here, and from now on keep this fact before you whenever you read the Bible, you cannot go far wrong. It's true that it talks about many other things (including man) but its main purpose is to tell us *who God is* and *what he does*.

Our problem is that we aren't so interested in God. We tend to use the Bible for other reasons: usually we pick it up when we need some consolation, for example, and we look for what will give us some hope and make us feel better in the middle of trying circumstances. Things will get better, we hope it will say. And when we *want* to see something in the Bible, we usually will — it's such a huge book and it's easy to twist its words to suit our purposes. So we end up with our favorite list of passages on consolation that we constantly turn to, while still knowing very little about what the Bible says about God.

The Bible is not about us primarily. We of course figure largely in the story of the Bible; God is always dealing with man in some way or another. But to focus on man alone while reading it is a great mistake and you will open yourself to all kinds of errors.

The Bible is not primarily a philosophy book, though there is philosophy in it. It is not a textbook on science or psychology or economics, though students of these disciplines would do well to study the Bible *first* before getting into their special interests — it would definitely keep them from going off into wrong directions.

No, the Bible is primarily about God. You need to keep this in mind whenever you pick it up to read it. The first question that ought to be on your lips when you read *any* passage is this: what does this tell me about God? Look and look until you find it; it is always there. You will never understand that passage correctly until you find out what it teaches you about God. Until you do, you will either get nothing out of the text or you will get the wrong point.

God-Centered Ministry

Let's put it like this: *the most important thing that you must do in life is to learn the truth about God.* Your job, your education, your family, your friends, your possessions are all secondary in importance; you could easily lose all of that and still find eternal life. Yet if you shove aside the knowledge of God and pursue "more important" things, you will find that you have made the greatest mistake of your life. David knew that when he led the nation Israel back to God.

> Whom have I in Heaven but you? And earth has nothing I desire besides you. (Psalm 73:25)

It's a logical yet tragic problem. The Bible is about God. So if we don't understand the Bible (to the degree that Paul describes it – the "deep truths of the faith" – 1 Timothy 3:9) then we won't understand God. That leaves only man to preach about – our duties, our responsibilities, our works, our glory.

Since the church is founded on the Bible, its entire ministry is therefore about God. The church will do no good to anybody if it doesn't center its worship, works, prayers, and teachings on God. This is, in fact, one of the biggest reasons that people are turning away from the church by the millions. They may not be able to articulate it, but that *something missing* that they feel in their hearts is God himself. Churches, for some reason, have settled down to a man-centered religion and they like it that way.

Man-centered religion

Man is so self-centered, so focused on himself, so wrapped up in his own little world, that this might be a difficult concept to grasp. *Your religion is either focused on yourself or on God.*

With a *man-centered* religion, instead of focusing on God and his works, the focus is on man and what we are supposed to do. **There is no hope, no salvation in this form of ministry.** If all we can offer people looking for help is more effort on their part, we haven't helped them at all. We are pointing them to the wrong savior – themselves.

Here are a few characteristics of a man-centered religion.

God-Centered Ministry

- **Moralisms** – What I mean by this is a list of do's and don'ts that you pressure people into observing. Do this and this and this, and don't do that and that and that.

This is appealing to people on several fronts. First, it looks as if the Bible really is set up this way. Morals and ethics fill the Bible from front to back. The Ten Commandments stand guard over the whole book, and all the writers after Moses take us back to that Law and make sure we get the point. All of society understands that Western systems of morality came primarily from the Bible's teachings.

Second, we love to swing into action to solve problems. Just give us a glimmer of hope that our own efforts can make the problem go away and we will begin immediately on whatever you tell us to do.

So preachers and teachers will give people what they want by boiling down the entire Bible to a handy list of morals for them to observe. For example, we are told to –

- Have the **patience** of Job.
- Have the **faith** of Abraham.
- Have the **courage** of David.
- Be **holy** like Jesus.
- Avoid the **lusts** of the flesh like Joseph.
- Be a **witness** like Paul.

You have probably heard many more. In fact, most of the sermons and lessons you've heard over the years have probably been mostly along this line.

The problem is that we can't do these things. Even the people mentioned in this list (with the exception of Jesus)

God-Centered Ministry

would testify that, in themselves, they could never do God's will on their own – only because *God* enabled them to do the impossible did they find themselves able to obey him. The secret was to get in touch with the God who has the answers. Though we *are* told to be like this, the Bible never leads us to believe that we can do it without God!

- **Psychology and counseling** – Sermon after sermon could easily be duplicated in the psychiatrist's chair. Are you lonely? Fellowship will lift your spirits. Do you have a problem getting along with your neighbor? Be a loving person – the problem between you and your neighbor will then solve itself. Do you need help sorting out your daily responsibilities? We can teach you how to be a Christian homemaker, a Christian businessman, a Christian athlete, a Christian parent – follow this advice, and life will become more pleasant and fulfilling for you.

It sounds as if preachers are simply giving counseling sessions from the pulpit. In fact, take out the occasional (and usually meaningless) references to God, and these sermons could easily be transcripts of psychologists of *any* religious faith telling their clients how to live a happier life. People are filling the mega-churches who cater to their home needs with family counseling sermons. There's nothing peculiarly Christian about the message; it could be just as well delivered by a Jewish rabbi or a Hindu swami.

On the other hand, a peculiarly Christian sermon or lesson should give great offense to a non-believing psychiatrist. It should go contrary to established counseling principles, because it leads man to a God who doesn't do things man's way but by his own way – by the Truth, by the Spirit, by miracle and by command.

- **Social issues** – Man is a political creature, and preachers get caught up in current events just like everyone else. So it's tempting to focus on what's going

God-Centered Ministry

on in the world in one's "Bible" lesson. The justification for this is that the Bible supposedly speaks to current events and how Christians need to relate to what's happening around them.

So there are sermons on abortion, on women's rights, on the Presidential race, on wars, on gay marriage, on education, on entertainment (with specific movies or stars becoming the point of the sermon!) and on everything else going on under the sun.

It's true that the Bible does address all the issues of life. But it's not true that the Bible focuses on these issues. Our faith is not based on what we think of what is going on in the world; it is based on what we know about God. The same people who can write whole books on abortion, for example, don't know enough about the Old Testament to fill a sheet of paper! They would make learned professors on human rights in secular schools, but they don't make good pastors leading people back to God. There is a time to pronounce God's edict on man's behavior and society's morals and practices; but it's also far too easy to major on *that* instead of focusing on knowing God – which is the believer's chief concern and duty. (John 17:3)

- **<u>Lip service to God</u>** – While people keep focusing on minor issues like this, they like to think that they are doing God a service. So they use his name in their sermons – "God" and "Jesus" and the "Spirit" – like sprinkling salt and pepper on a meal. By doing this, evidently, they think that God will approve of what they are saying. It makes it seem like a Christian lesson.

So often preachers and teachers of the Bible will do what I call "name-dropping." In other words, they use God's name and Christ's name all through their lessons, but they don't give any content to the words. They tell us that "We must believe in Jesus!" without stopping to tell us anything about Jesus. Notice the simple grammar of this sentence.

We	**must believe in**	**Jesus**
subject	*action*	*object*

The subject of a sentence does the action upon the object. In this case, the people listening are encouraged to do the action; *they* are the subject, the main focus of the lesson. Jesus is simply the passive receiver of all the work that they are counseled to do. If you don't believe that this is typical of modern Bible lessons, keep track sometime of the speakers you hear and note what they are telling you to do.

Dropping God's name throughout the sermon like this isn't teaching us about God. It's dishonest, really – there is a world of information about God in the Bible begging us to study it, holding out life to us – but we're ignoring almost all of it and simply using God's name to grace our counseling sessions or social analyses. We aren't really conveying any new information *about God* when we use his name like this.

For example, we are told to believe in God. We emphasize the word "believe" because that's something that we can do, or so we think. We like activity. But very few people actually ask themselves the obvious question – what exactly are we supposed to believe *about* God? What is the content of our faith? What is it that we see there in him? Or are we not concerned with God himself – only in our own activity of "believing" or having faith?

We are told to be good – to follow the Ten Commandments, to live a righteous life as Jesus did. Has no one noticed that the Jews themselves failed to keep those Ten Commandments over a 1500 year training period? Did everyone miss the fact that, if Jesus is the only Perfect Man to have lived on earth, then we *can't* live as he did?

We are told to devote ourselves to the Lord, to love him with all of our hearts. Whom do we love? What is it in him that would capture the heart and make it want to be devoted to him? Where is the motivation, the fire that warms the heart to the work, the vision of who God is that so draws the human heart out to God and to nothing else? What is it about God that would take away our dread of him, our innate hatred of his ways?

These examples show that we really aren't talking about God – we're talking about ourselves. No amount of name-dropping, however, will make our sermons and lessons "Christ-centered" or "Bible-based."

The main objection to a man-centered religion is that **there is no salvation in it**. If there is a central message about man all through the Bible, from front to back, it is this – man is in a desperate situation. He has offended God, he has ruined himself and God's creation, he is physically dying and spiritually dead, and unless something drastic is done he is off to an eternal state of misery as the universe's most infamous convict. Our only hope is for something from *outside* man, *outside* his world, to come in and rescue him. In light of this theme, it's really misleading to tell people that their own actions are the answer to their problems.

All the faith in the world won't get us close to God. Only Jesus does that. All the courage in the world won't help us stand against the Enemy. Only Jesus can protect us. Go ahead and try to love God and man with all of your heart; you will find that somewhere, sometime, that love of yours will fail and you will fall back to the innate hatred, animosity, lust, rebellion and general contrariness that every human being has in himself.

> The LORD saw how great man's wickedness on the earth had become, and that every inclination of the

> thoughts of his heart was only evil all the time. (Genesis 6:5)
>
> There is not a righteous man on earth who does what is right and never sins. (Ecclesiastes 7:20)
>
> The heart is deceitful above all things and beyond cure. Who can understand it? (Jeremiah 17:9)
>
> So I find this law at work: When I want to do good, evil is right there with me. For in my inner being I delight in God's Law; but I see another law at work in the members of my body, waging war against the law of my mind and making me a prisoner of the law of sin at work within my members. What a wretched man I am! Who will rescue me from this body of death? (Romans 7:21-24)

If you don't give someone hope that a Person greater than they are has the power and determination to rescue them, they will end up with no hope – especially when they keep trying to do this Christianity thing and it doesn't work out.

When Jesus came to this world, he found the Jews bound by the same man-centered religion. Instead of learning the right lesson from their history, the Jews considered themselves experts in the Law and righteous enough to please God with their own works. We call this *legalism* – because the emphasis is not on God's grace and mercy to sinners, but expecting a reward from God, and entrance into Heaven, for our good works. When Jesus offered them a way of escape from their sins by his own righteousness and his blood sacrifice to cover their sins, they rejected him completely. God's response to the Jews was to cut them off from the Vine, to take the Gospel to the Gentiles.

God-centered religion

A God-centered ministry, on the other hand, actually turns to God and starts studying *him*.

God-Centered Ministry

This might seem like a strange exercise at first, but its strangeness only proves the point. We are so used to thinking about ourselves that we are at first confused and uneasy when we try to think about *only* God. We feel that we've done Bible study when we see ourselves, or something that relates to our personal situation, in the passage. The saints in Bible times, however, were masters at studying God.

Those of you who have been married (or have thought about it!) know exactly what I mean. When you found the one you loved, you didn't focus on how *you* felt, or what *you* did – you focused exclusively on how the object of your affections looked or what they did. His or her every look, and every move, fascinated you, captivated you, held you in a helpless wonder.

It's interesting that the Bible puts our worship of God in the same terms. Like a marriage, God becomes our Lover, our Husband, our Provider. The Bible talks about the beauty of Christ, the faithfulness of the Father, the majesty and glory of God on his throne. We read of his works and the ways he does things. The more clearly we see him, the easier it is to be fascinated with this God and fall in love with him. Quickly we lose sight of ourselves as we fill our eyes and hearts and minds with the knowledge of God.

This is, after all, our duty. Jesus said it plainly.

> ***Love*** the Lord your God with all your heart and with all your soul and with all your mind. This is the first and greatest commandment. (Matthew 22:37)

Now love doesn't happen in ignorance. You can't love your wife or husband without knowing anything about them! In the same way, you will find that, until you learn a good deal about God, you are going to feel anything but love for him. Sinners don't love a holy God; rebels don't love a powerful King; immoral wretches don't love a righteous Judge. This is, in fact, what many so-called Christians will discover at the Gates of Heaven. He doesn't like them, and they're not going to like him.

God-Centered Ministry

> Not everyone who says to me, 'Lord, Lord,' will enter the kingdom of Heaven, but only he who does the will of my Father who is in Heaven. Many will say to me on that day, 'Lord, Lord, did we not prophesy in your name, and in your name drive out demons and perform many miracles?' Then I will tell them plainly, 'I never knew you. Away from me, you evildoers!' (Matthew 7:21-23)

Look, for example, at the Psalms. Here is a wealth of information about God. In Psalm 105 is a list of important truths about the Lord that we need to know – data that is worth our time to mine out of Scripture, like gold.

> Give thanks to the LORD, call on his Name; make known among the nations what he has done. Sing to him, sing praise to him; tell of all his wonderful acts. Glory in his holy Name; let the hearts of those who seek the LORD rejoice. Look to the LORD and his strength; seek his face always. Remember the wonders he has done, his miracles, and the judgments he pronounced, O descendants of Abraham his servant, O sons of Jacob, his chosen ones. He is the LORD our God; his judgments are in all the earth. He remembers his covenant forever, the word he commanded, for a thousand generations, the covenant he made with Abraham, the oath he swore to Isaac. He confirmed it to Jacob as a decree, to Israel as an everlasting covenant. (Psalm 105:1-10)

One day I stumbled across this passage and realized that the years of Bible study that God had led me to do focused exactly on these themes – and here they were, recommended to me by Scripture! The Name of the LORD, the Covenant, his judgments, his works and miracles – these were the subjects he had led me to focus on in my studies. It was a great confirmation that God wanted me to learn about *him* when I study the Bible.

God-Centered Ministry

It's amazing how preachers and teachers can miss this point. ***The whole purpose of the Bible is to reveal God.*** God is on every page. There is no other book under Heaven given for this purpose. Whatever we learn and know about God comes solely from the Bible, and all books which supposedly teach us about God must get its information only from the Bible in order to claim the label "truth." So, when we study the Bible, if we see who he is or what he does, we got the right point; otherwise we're missing the whole point.

Once we get the right idea of the purpose of the Bible – and pastors and teachers start focusing on God for a change – the rest of the ministry of the church will start straightening out. The sight of the holy God will humble us, teach us the fear of him, and cause us to look into the perfect righteousness that will please him. Praise and worship will center on God; what we learn from the Bible will move our hearts to give him thanks for what he is, and motivate us to pray for his presence, work, ways and treasures. When we use our gifts for the benefit of others, it won't be a matter of what I can do for you but what Christ can do for you through me. The church will start waiting on God to do his part, once they learn that God's works are worth waiting for.

How can we tell?

A God-centered ministry is going to have definite results. You can try to focus on God by bringing the sermons and lessons around to the subject of God, but the church may not be gripped with the reality of God yet. A man-centered ministry is hard to get rid of. But when the attitudes and actions of the congregation are starting to change, you know you're finally getting somewhere.

- *A longing for holiness* – You can't spend much time around God without having some sort of reaction to his utter holiness. If the church focuses on God in a powerful way, and the Spirit brings home the reality of what is being taught, then the people are going to start taking God more seriously in their lives. They are going to be thoroughly convinced of his calling them out of the world and into his presence. They will be in awe of his majesty. They will

God-Centered Ministry

humble themselves before him, not because they are told to but because they can't help but worship this God they've never seen before in this light. A holy awe, a new dedication, a new zeal will grip the congregation as it basks in the light of the Almighty.

- *A love for his kingdom* – Again, if you find yourself in the presence of God, you are going to react to the King in one of two ways. Either you will completely surrender to him and start doing his will, or you will rebel and get as far away as possible. The ones who don't like God will leave soon when they feel the power of the throne from Heaven making irresistible demands on their lives. Those who are becoming holy will surrender their will to the will of the King and start learning ways to please him. There will be a renewed interest in his published will – the Bible.

- *A true perspective on ourselves* – As God's light shines on us, we start seeing what we really are. Pride crumbles before the Master. Just as the tax collector couldn't even raise his head before the King, so church members will shed their arrogance and independent attitude and be amazed at the mercy of Christ toward such sinners as they. They will see others as better than themselves. They will feel the pain of even the least sins toward both God and man. They will start to appreciate the cure for their souls and apply continually to the throne of grace and mercy.

- **Total dependence on him** – Beggars know how to come before power and wealth – with open hands. The more the church sees the majesty and glory of God, the more they realize that, in comparison, they've been "wretched, pitiful, poor, blind and naked." They want the spiritual treasures in Christ; they want his power and wisdom; they will not rest until Christ is living in them, "the power of the Gospel." Even when they have nothing in this world, they will rest confident in what God gives them from his throne.

These are good signs that the ministry of a church is God-centered and the people are taking God seriously. The Mission is being accomplished.

Prayer – how to approach God

There's an excellent "barometer" in the life of the church that can tell us how spiritually healthy everyone is – the prayers. If prayer is simply a mechanical thing that people do, if they don't really look for answers from God but fully intend to do what they want whether God hears their prayers or not, then this will be plain to see. They'll have an arrogant, independent attitude in their prayers, as if they're telling God how to run his Kingdom. On the other hand, if people have a vision of God that humbles and awes them, that's going to come out in the *way* they approach him in prayer.

God requires his people to come to him with a certain attitude. Pride will get nowhere with him! A humble attitude, ready to listen instead of "uttering the speech of fools," looking to God for what we can't do for ourselves – this moves God to answer our prayers. Notice these six "essentials of prayer" in the Psalms.

- **Pray according to his Word**

    Do good to your servant according to your Word, O LORD. (Psalm 119:65)

    We have to pray, as Jesus told us, "in Spirit and in **truth**." (John 4:23-24) The Bible reveals who God is; without that, how could we possibly understand how to come to God, or what to say to him? Through the Bible we learn what is on God's heart: we learn what he is like, what he wants to see in us, how he feels about his world, and his future plans.

    What we often do, however, is pray whatever comes into our heads at the time! It's no wonder that we don't get answers when we don't take the time first to find out what God wants to talk to us about. Before God will listen to us, we have to get on the same "wavelength," so to speak. We have to get familiar with the issues that God wants to work on, and they have to become important to us too. These are, after all, things that pertain to our salvation! And in

God's eyes, our salvation is the most important work on earth.

So when we pray, we have to open the Bible. There God talks to us about what is on his heart. In it he tells us what he sees in our hearts that needs changing; through the Bible he trains us for battle in this world; he lays out the resources in his Word that we will need to get ready for Heaven. When we read about these things, *if* we are his children, we also will realize how important they are – and so ***that's*** *what we ask for in prayer.*

If you don't use the Word in prayer, God won't listen, and you could very well be talking to someone else (Satan, for example – see John 8:43-44) who would be more than happy to "answer" your prayers – since they will be based on your own desires and the world's "wisdom," instead of God's truth.

- **Start with God's Name**

    Hear us, O Shepherd of Israel, you who lead Joseph like a flock. (Psalm 80:1)

When we want to talk to someone, we first use their name. This is because we want the attention of a particular person, not anybody who happens to be standing nearby. So when you want something from the God of the Bible, the first thing you have to do is call on his Name. (Joel 2:32) Right away you are singling out a particular God from among many: you want the God of Israel, the Father of the Lord Jesus Christ, the Creator, the Redeemer. When you call his Name, you are putting an "address" on your letter so that other "gods" of this world can't intercept your prayer.

The names of God reveal what he is like and what kinds of things he does. When we look over his many names, we will see one in particular that perfectly answers the need we have. For example, the "Light from Heaven" shows us the path to take in this world and gives us wisdom to solve our problems.

Using the Name of God in prayer means more than just ending up with "In Jesus' name, Amen" – it's childish, or even superstitious, to think that that phrase alone will suffice. The Name should be the subject of our prayer, the thing about God that we are asking for. We need to pray his Name *all through* the prayer, from beginning to end! This is, in fact, how the Apostles prayed.

- **Pray in the Spirit**

   One thing I ask of the LORD, this is what I seek: that I may dwell in the house of the LORD all the days of my life, to gaze upon the beauty of the LORD and to seek him in his temple. (Psalm 27:4)

The Spirit does two things for us: he *reveals* the spiritual world of God to us (1 Corinthians 2:9-10), and he *empowers* us to live with spiritual resources from that world (Acts 1:8). All through the Bible we see the Spirit doing these two things for the people of God, because they need this spiritual insight and power to do the things that God requires of them.

That includes prayer. In order to pray, you have to leave this physical world, so to speak, and come into God's presence in Heaven. Remember that Jesus said, "God is Spirit, and his worshipers must worship in **Spirit** and in truth." (John 4:23) You have to be able to deal with spiritual issues, and handle spiritual answers that God gives you. To do this, you have to be "walking in the Spirit" (Galatians 5:24-25) and capable of using the treasures of Heaven to solve earth's problems.

You can tell when you're not praying in the Spirit – when you're asking for something that unbelievers are also interested in. They have no interest in God from a spiritual point of view; they only want more of this world's treasures. So when you pray as a child of God longing for the things of Heaven, they don't understand you and they are repelled by the thought.

> The man without the Spirit does not accept the things that come from the Spirit of God, for they are foolishness to him, and he cannot understand them, because they are spiritually discerned. (1 Corinthians 2:14)

- **Pray with faith**

For you have delivered me from death and my feet from stumbling, that I may walk before God in the light of life. (Psalm 56:13)

Faith is being able to see God's spiritual world; what was once a tradition and a story in the Bible suddenly becomes real to a person through faith. They see with their spiritual eyes, because the Spirit reveals it to them – and now they know that such things are real. Their spiritual eyes are open and now they *know* God. (John 3:3-8)

When this happens, the world we live in takes on a whole new light. Now we know that God's promises are more powerful than the problems we have. God does impossible things; he overturns this world's obstacles with overwhelming spiritual forces. Through faith we can grasp how precious God's world is (more than anything in this world), and that nothing can or will stop God from what he wants to do. Faith enables us to follow Jesus who can move mountains.

And if we truly have faith, we can wait for answers – because we know, ***first***, that nothing short of an answer from God will be sufficient; and ***second***, that he *will* do what he promises. Waiting on him, come what may, is one of the surest proofs that we have true faith.

- **Pray for his will**

    The LORD has established his throne in Heaven, and his kingdom rules over all. Praise the LORD, you his angels, you mighty ones who do his bidding, who obey his word. Praise the LORD, all his Heavenly hosts, you his servants who do his will. Praise the LORD, all his works everywhere in his dominion. Praise the LORD, O my soul. (Psalm 103:19-22)

God is the King. We have to learn that first about him if we want to get anywhere with him. He made the world, he rules over it, and he expects just one thing from all of his creatures: the service of obedience.

You aren't going to tell God anything that he doesn't already know. Nor are your ideas better than his. The purpose of prayer, therefore, is to *change you*. Through prayer, you learn what God is like, you learn what his will is, your heart starts burning with the same emotions that God has toward certain issues, and you begin to want what he wants. Then you are in a position to receive what he promises in his Word. Prayer is getting yourself in the right spiritual position to receive what he wants to give you from his treasures in Heaven. Until this submission to his will happens in your heart, you would only use answers to prayer to satisfy the lusts of your heart anyway. (James 4:3)

- **Pray for his glory**

    All you have made will praise you, O LORD; your saints will extol you. They will tell of the glory of your kingdom and speak of your might, so that all men may know of your mighty acts and the glorious splendor of your kingdom. (Psalm 145:10-12)

The word "glory" means "who gets the credit." Prayer should be a time when we tell God how much we appreciate him. But man is so used to getting glory for himself; he is his most favorite subject! We little realize how much God has given us – and how much he takes care of us every day. Prayer is the time to focus on that.

God gets almost no glory for what he does. Read the newspaper and see if it tells how God fed his creatures today, raising up nations and bringing them down, judged people's hearts and built his church. Though he does all of this daily, almost nobody pays attention to that fact. But he wants credit for it – because *God's* works are the things that make the world and the Church work.

We need to pray for two things: *first*, that God would do things that nobody else can do, things that will get people's attention and make them fear and worship him for a change. *Second*, that we might become less and he might become greater. He likes worshipers who understand the importance of making him the center of their lives. Our goal in life is to depend on him alone.

People who pray like this prove that they really are entering into the presence of God when they worship him. God's glory overshadows them, reminds them of proper protocol in his presence, and emboldens them to take hold of spiritual treasures instead of the empty things of this world.

The Churches in Revelation

Each of the letters to the seven churches starts out with a unique picture of Jesus. It describes something about his appearance, or something of the work that he does. For example, the first letter starts like this:

God-Centered Ministry

To the angel of the church in Ephesus write: These are the words of him who holds the seven stars in his right hand and walks among the seven golden lampstands. (Revelation 2:1)

This isn't just an interesting picture. This is valuable information about Christ that this church in particular needs to focus on. He holds each of the churches in his hands, he is telling them. He controls their destiny, their ministry, their very existence. They each exist to serve him. If they don't serve him then he can snuff out their light if he so chooses. In fact, if they don't start focusing on him – their "first love" – as they did at the beginning, he threatens to take away their lampstand and they will no longer be allowed to be a witness for him. In other words, he will shut down their church.

Every church's ministry vitally depends on getting a grip on who Jesus is. It is paramount that Christians become a God-centered, Christ-centered church, according to what the Word tells them about God. If they start taking seriously what Jesus is doing, then they can cooperate with him as he is building his Kingdom. Otherwise, in their ignorance of him, they will end up working against him – and he'll be forced to put them out of his way.

Summary

The only way that a church can accomplish its Mission is to turn its attention to God and learn of him. God has to become the center of that church's ministry. The entire Bible is about God, for good reason – we need to learn as much of him as we can to make faith and a holy life possible, and it requires both the Old and New Testaments to adequately explain God. A man-centered religion, which so many churches are good at, will kill a church – there's no life or salvation in it. It's time for the churches to sit down at Jesus' feet and learn of him.

Government

*Our Father in Heaven, hallowed be your Name, your
kingdom come, your will be done on earth as it is in Heaven.*
(Matthew 6:9-10)

Isn't it strange that, when we pray, we often don't mean what we say.

The average American Christian would be appalled if our Father in Heaven actually answered this prayer. We don't want to live in a kingdom – we prefer a democracy in which we can express our opinions and put in our vote. Our idea of fairness and justice means that every one of us – even in the church – has a say in what happens. Our democratic system has given us the perfect setup to live as we please, calling no man master. If God actually imposed a Kingdom upon us (with all its ramifications), we would cry like babies. I've seen it happen.

The irony of the modern church is that Jesus has gone back to Heaven to sit on his **throne** – we become Christians by calling him "**Lord**" (Romans 10:9) – and yet we demand complete freedom to live exactly as we please. We don't want anybody, or any institution, telling us what to think or how to live. Such an independent attitude doesn't go over very well with the King.

Christ the King

Jesus is setting up a Kingdom – not a democracy. He alone intends to be King. His will prevails. If the church is an open democracy where everybody rules, then it's not a Kingdom. It's as simple as that.

We Americans need special instruction on the nature and operations of kingdoms. First of all, it's a hierarchy – Jesus is on top, which means that he has absolute power and authority over everyone beneath him. And all the rest of us *are* beneath him, at various levels of authority and responsibility.

Government

If you truly understand the problem of man and God's solution to fix the problem, you shouldn't be surprised to learn of the system that God set up to fix the problem. The problem is sin – rebellion against God's rule. The solution is to change the heart of man to submit to God's rule over him. Therefore, we start out (do you remember this at the beginning of your spiritual walk?) by acknowledging that Christ is Lord over us. That is, he is a King, and you are his subject. He rules, you obey.

> Therefore let all Israel be assured of this: God has made this Jesus, whom you crucified, both Lord and Christ. (Acts 2:36)

> That if you confess with your mouth, "Jesus is Lord," and believe in your heart that God raised him from the dead, you will be saved. (Romans 10:9)

> That at the name of Jesus every knee should bow, in heaven and on earth and under the earth, and every tongue confess that Jesus Christ is Lord, to the glory of God the Father. (Philippians 2:10-11)

> So then, just as you received Christ Jesus as Lord, continue to live in him. (Colossians 2:6)

This brings each person back to the original position of humanity: are you going to renounce your rebellion against God, repent of your lawlessness, humble yourself before his throne, give up living your own way, and start doing his will alone? If you are, you begin the process of fixing what Adam broke.

It would be nice if this were all that was necessary, but the Old Testament teaches us that it rarely carries off so blissfully. We may say that we submit to God; but when God is invisible, and we go back to work the next day, and sin is so easy to do and the opportunities for sin abound – we usually forget our fine-sounding words of devotion and go back to our own ways. In this world we need a **government** to remind us of God and to enforce his rule over us. The Israelites were living proof that it is all but impossible to live in God's Kingdom successfully without outward helps. Hence the need for King David after the 400 years of lawless disaster under the Judges:

> In those days Israel had no king; everyone did as he saw fit.
> (Judges 21:25)

Jesus, being the Son of David, of course would set up a Kingdom to rule over his subjects and bring the entire Kingdom under the Law of God – "just as his father David had done." You can find the rules and laws of his Kingdom outlined in the Sermon on the Mount – Matthew 5-7. You can find the *organization* of his Kingdom in this Ephesians passage, as well as other passages.

> But to each one of us grace has been given as Christ apportioned it. This is why it says: "When he ascended on high, he led captives in his train and gave gifts to men." ... *It was he who gave some to be apostles, some to be prophets, some to be evangelists, and some to be pastors and teachers.* (Ephesians 4:7-8, 11)

In fact, he has pulled the Church together to form his Body, of which he is the Head. Each Christian is an important part of the whole, and has a responsibility given him by Christ to perform a vital function for the well-being of the whole. Christ directs, we obey, we all live. This is the basis of the spiritual gifts that we've been given to serve the Body of Christ.

In Christ's government there is only one Head – Christ himself. Democracy has no place in the Church. We aren't supposed to vote on morality, or the Word, or salvation issues, or what the church needs to do in its work of the Kingdom – we are supposed to seek his will and do that *with no questions*. His is an absolute dictatorship; he is, as Peter describes, a despot (δεσπότης – 2 Peter 2:1) – in the good sense. He is not interested in our opinions; we've messed up our lives following our own will and ideas. He is interested only in our obedience. Disobedience brings condemnation. (See Matthew 25 for examples of man's opinionated excuses and Christ's kingly wrath.)

Government

Whatever government the Church will have, therefore, will be a system of passing down Christ's will to all the members – it is *not* letting them choose their own ways! No wonder, therefore, that the Apostles and Prophets (the *source* of the Scriptures, the printed will of Christ) and pastors and teachers (the *means* whereby the Scriptures are given to the Church) figure so largely in the structure of the Church's operations. Once you have this principle down, it's just a matter of learning God's will, doing it, and correcting those who fail to carry out God's will.

In David's day there were certain men who understood the need for a king who would set up God's rule over Israel. These were the famous "mighty men" who joined David in the wilderness. Their goal was to help make David king, to establish his kingdom, to help him rule over Israel according to God's Law.

> … Men of Issachar, who understood the times and knew what Israel should do. (1 Chronicles 12:32)
>
> All these were fighting men who volunteered to serve in the ranks. They came to Hebron fully determined to make David king over all Israel. All the rest of the Israelites were also of one mind to make David king. (1 Chronicles 12:38)

This is precisely what the leaders of a church are called to do – to extend the rule of Christ, the son of David, to the church; to implement his policies, his will, his power, his influence, his treasures in the life of the church.

Why is a Kingdom better than a democracy? Because only Jesus can take care of us. The nature of our problems and needs is beyond the ability of men to solve. Jesus alone knows our weaknesses, our exact situations, the right timing for supporting us. In fact, he has to do this for everyone in his Body – your needs aren't the only items on his agenda! The affairs of running the Kingdom of God are staggering to try to imagine, yet Jesus is running it perfectly. It would be fatal to turn over the affairs of the Kingdom to man. We are so limited in our knowledge and power that it's a mercy Jesus is doing it for us. *So, we do not interfere in how he chooses to run his Kingdom.* We do it his way.

Ways that Christ rules

How does one distinguish whether Christ is ruling in a church or just man? At first glance it may appear that people are running the show in the church – song leaders, preachers and teachers, deacons and elders, committee members. These are what we immediately see. But is the Lord really running things? How can we tell?

There are at least three ways we can tell if Jesus is the head of a church or whether people have pushed him out of the picture.

- *He rules through his Word* – The Church has various tools and methods for achieving the goal of bringing sinners into submission before God, but the most powerful one is the Word of God. Again, people use the Bible for all sorts of things – it lends itself to comfort, hope, encouragement, and other ministrations that appeal to the aching heart. But first and foremost the Bible is a manual for addressing man's central problem – his sin. Many have developed the ability to read around the sections that confront them as rebellious sinners and they head straight for the promises. However, that won't help them at all on Judgment Day. They must face the problem head-on. If you don't see yourself as a sinner, then you have not yet seen yourself, nor do you understand the purpose of the Bible.

  The Bible is designed to do several things for us:

  All Scripture is God-breathed and is useful for teaching, rebuking, correcting and training in righteousness, so that the man of God may be thoroughly equipped for every good work. (2 Timothy 3:16-17)

  Note what functions it serves us –

Government

- **Teaching** – because we do not yet know what we need to know about either God, ourselves, our problem or the solution.

- **Rebuking** – because we keep sinning in many ways, and we need to face that fact and stop.

- **Correcting** – because we keep taking the wrong road and have to be continually shown the right way to go to follow Christ.

- **Training in righteousness** – because we have a long way to go before we are anywhere near the righteousness of Christ.

None of these functions appeal to our pride, all of them can be and are painful to go through, and yet they are necessary for every single person in the Church. In fact, if this isn't happening in a person's life when they study the Bible, they are using it to no purpose. You can, for example, use a geography book as a source of pretty pictures; but that's not its purpose. It has pretty pictures – but you are supposed to learn the principles of geography and master the knowledge. In the same way, people have their favorite passages underlined all through the Bible – usually the promises, almost never the humbling descriptions of their crippling sins and how to overcome them. You will never be saved from sin at that rate.

The old divines used to say that there are two main functions in Church – preaching and prayer. Whatever else there may be in your church (and unfortunately we sinners like to multiply functions in an effort to avoid or water down the two main ones) we need the preaching of the Word to convict us of our sin (John 16:8), and the ministry of prayer to appeal to God to change us from sinners to saints (Luke 18:13). In fact, if all you had in your church were these two functions, that would be all you really need to get ready for Heaven. The rest of what happens in churches nowadays is mostly just psychology and sociology and has no direct relevance to the task.

Government

Christ, as the Head of the Church, has of course provided just what we need for the ministry of the Word in the Church.

> It was he who gave some to be apostles, some to be prophets, some to be evangelists, and some to be pastors and teachers, to prepare God's people for works of service, so that the body of Christ may be built up until we all reach unity in the faith and in the knowledge of the Son of God and become mature, attaining to the whole measure of the fullness of Christ. (Ephesians 4:11-13)

The Apostles and Prophets gave us the Bible itself. The pastors and teachers take that Word and impress it on the hearers' lives. The process involved is *training* – a little-used concept in today's church, but desperately needed. The result is –

> You were taught, with regard to your former way of life, to put off your old self, which is being corrupted by its deceitful desires; to be made new in the attitude of your minds; and to put on the new self, created to be like God in true righteousness and holiness. (Ephesians 4:22-24)

If the Word is faithfully taught as the King's will, and the members are listening and taking it to heart – in other words, they are changing from sinners to saints – then Jesus really does rule in that church.

- *He rules through his Spirit* – Jesus promised us that when he went back to Heaven he would send the Spirit to indwell us. It is conceivable that a person could read the Bible and learn its teachings, and yet not know the reality of God's spiritual world. But when a Christian has the Spirit of Christ in him, there is no way he can deny the reality of God – the Spirit brings him into the presence of God so that he can see God's glory, hear his voice, and love him.

Government

The first step is to change the heart. The best passage that describes this event is in the Prophets.

> I will sprinkle clean water on you, and you will be clean; I will cleanse you from all your impurities and from all your idols. I will give you a new heart and put a new spirit in you; I will remove from you your heart of stone and give you a heart of flesh. And I will put my Spirit in you and move you to follow my decrees and be careful to keep my laws. (Ezekiel 36:25-27)

The first sign, therefore, of the presence of Christ is that a person's heart changes – and *that* is the basis of a changed life. He no longer loves sin or this world; he loves God and the next world. He is humble before God and obedient, ready to follow the Lord's will in his Word. He changes his lifestyle to please the Lord instead of his own lusts and desires. His heart fills with the fruit of the Spirit – a sure sign that there's spiritual life there.

> But the fruit of the Spirit is love, joy, peace, patience, kindness, goodness, faithfulness, gentleness and self-control. Against such things there is no law. Those who belong to Christ Jesus have crucified the sinful nature with its passions and desires. (Galatians 5:22-24)

Wise church leaders know about this. They know they can't change people's hearts – it's not their job to do that. Their duty is to preach the Word of Christ and then pray and wait for the Spirit to do the rest of the work. And they will make sure that they don't hinder the free operation of the gifts of the Spirit, because it's through these functions that the Lord develops his people's faith and life.

- *He rules through Worship* – To be exact, worship is the *result* of two things: preaching the Word as Christ's will, and the Spirit making God's spiritual world real to his people. But we can add worship as another aspect to the life of the church because it's a necessary outlet for the other two. As we saw in the previous chapter, it *is* possible to bottle up the work of the Spirit in people's hearts by turning Christianity into a man-centered, introspective religion that puts the Spirit's fire out.

Worship is, as we've seen, humbling oneself before God. We will only truly worship God if we *know* him (the result of teaching the Word faithfully) and *see* him (the result of the Spirit opening our eyes to him). And we need to worship him for several reasons: ***first***, we see his glory, his overwhelming holiness, his profound wisdom, his love and faithfulness that knows no limits, his power that overwhelms. That sight will awe and terrify anybody, as the examples in the Bible show us clearly. ***Second***, we immediately see what we are in light of this God. Our sin is too much to bear, our ignorance is embarrassing and painful, our self-will and streak of independence is a dark stain in God's pure light. Who can stand before God in light of all that? ***Third***, we see how amazing God's love is in giving us a way of escape from our sin and weakness. The vision of Christ, if truly seen for what it is, is like a starving man seeing a feast laid out before him, or a dying man seeing the fountain of life. The treasures of Heaven are so appropriate for what I need! Why would Christ do such things for an unworthy sinner like me? ***Fourth***, we know exactly what we have to do – plead for that mercy and love of God in Christ given for us. We need this; we are desperate for this; we are reduced to helpless beggars, with nothing to offer God in return. But we are called by God to come, take and eat.

Hopefully you can get a sense of what true worship is from this picture. It can happen silently, it can happen in prayer, both individual and corporate, it can happen during the sermon or Sunday School lesson, it can happen in praise and song. But the reality of coming before God like this completes the circle and proves beyond all doubt that Jesus rules in his church.

Government

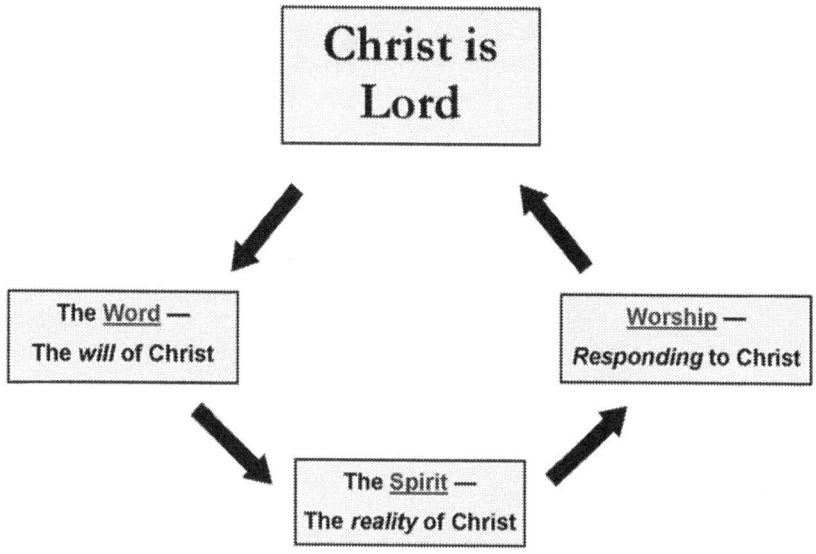

Christ rules in his church

The Hierarchy

There are three levels of government in Christ's Kingdom.

- *First*, the **Apostles and Prophets** got their authority from God himself. Their duty was more than simply to wander around the world preaching and starting churches. God gave them the **Word**, they wrote it down, and they passed it on to us. We now possess the Word of God by their efforts. That's why the work of the Prophets and Apostles is so fundamental to the work of the Church.

> Consequently, you are no longer foreigners and aliens, but fellow citizens with God's people and members of God's household, ***built on the foundation of the apostles and prophets,*** with Christ Jesus himself as the chief cornerstone. (Ephesians 2:19-20)

Government

We honor that authority by learning and doing what they passed on to us from Christ. These are the very words of God. In other words (in case it hasn't hit you yet) *we do not deviate from the truth of the Bible*. We are not free to add to it or subtract from it. It is true just as it stands. It doesn't need our present culture to improve it. It is truth for all ages, all people everywhere, just as it reads. People who would water down or do away with passages in the Bible are enemies of Christ – and the church needs to identify them as such.

This Word – both Old and New Testaments – is what God has given his church through all ages to be saved from sin and death. It is perfectly adequate to do that job. It is the full statement of our faith and practice; we need nothing else for the purpose. And with the work of the Spirit, all of God's people can understand its message and be saved – they need nothing else but the Word of God. [1]

- *Second*, **pastors and teachers** are also assigned to their jobs – Christ gave these functions to the Church for her growth and well-being. Where did we get the notion that these functions in the church are hired positions? To treat a pastor or teacher in Christ's church as an employee is to reject Christ's authority. Pastors usually get a "paycheck," but that doesn't make the shepherd an employee of the sheep – such an idea is absurd. Pastors and teachers are Christ's workers, shepherds assigned to the job of caring for Christ's flock. The "pay" that a pastor receives is compensation for his hard work for the flock, and imposed on that flock by the Lord of the Church.

> The elders who direct the affairs of the church well are worthy of double honor, especially those whose work is preaching and teaching. For the Scripture says, "Do not muzzle the ox while it is treading out the grain," and "The worker deserves his wages." (1 Timothy 5:17-18)

At any rate, shepherds are answerable to the Chief Shepherd. They are to do the job he gave them to do, as he describes it in his

---

[1] A fascinating example of Jesus "doing as his father David had done" is found in the Gospels that show us Christ choosing his disciples. He was literally collecting the "materials" for the spiritual Temple he is building; they are the "foundation" that he would build his church upon. See Matthew 4:18-22.

Government

Word. To hold them responsible to do what church members dream up as a replacement for God's job description in the Bible is to shackle them with trivia that prevents them from doing *Christ's* will.

> So the Twelve gathered all the disciples together and said, "It would not be right for us to neglect the ministry of the Word of God in order to wait on tables. Brothers, choose seven men from among you who are known to be full of the Spirit and wisdom. We will turn this responsibility over to them and will give our attention to prayer and the ministry of the Word." (Acts 6:2-4)

Their allegiance and obedience is *upward* in the hierarchy, to Christ – their duties downward to the flock.

> Be shepherds of God's flock that is under your care, serving as overseers – not because you must, but because you are willing, as God wants you to be; not greedy for money, but eager to serve; not lording it over those entrusted to you, but being examples to the flock. And when the Chief Shepherd appears, you will receive the crown of glory that will never fade away. (1 Peter 5:1-4)

The authority of a leader is not an empty concept. He has the right and the duty to use the Word of God boldly in the church – applying it to people's hearts as necessary. If he shies away from his duty to confront sinners with their sin, he isn't doing them any favors and he is opening up the whole church to confusion about how serious sin is. And if he beats the sheep, the Chief Shepherd is going to have harsh words for him. So at times he has to be firm and confrontational, and at other times gentle and compassionate. His goal at all times, however, is to lead the flock to salvation in Christ. We *have* to take them seriously – they are Christ's representatives.

> I will give you the keys of the kingdom of Heaven; whatever you bind on earth will be bound in Heaven, and whatever you loose on earth will be loosed in Heaven. (Matthew 16:19)

Government

> This is why I write these things when I am absent, that when I come I may not have to be harsh in my use of authority – the authority the Lord gave me for building you up, not for tearing you down. (2 Corinthians 13:10)

The leaders of the church are responsible for *teaching* and *discipline*. They are to use the Word alone for teaching; as we've seen, God's people need only God's Word, and all of God's Word, to be saved and prepared for Heaven. The leaders are responsible to become well-trained in the Bible so that they can give the flock what it needs.

> Therefore every teacher of the Law who has been instructed about the kingdom of Heaven is like the owner of a house who brings out of his storeroom new treasures as well as old. (Matthew 13:52)

> Do your best to present yourself to God as one approved, a workman who does not need to be ashamed and who correctly handles the word of truth. (2 Timothy 2:15)

Discipline involves many things – correcting troublemakers in the church is only one of its aspects. Perhaps if you think of the military you will begin to appreciate its fuller meaning. In order to prepare soldiers for battle, the officers make the recruits drill and practice and drill and practice until they can do it in their sleep! This continual training is for a purpose: on the battlefield, a soldier has to the *right* thing *immediately*, or he will die. There is no time to study in the middle of a battle. The right action has to be instinct. In the same way, the leaders of the church must train the members in the truths and practice of Christianity so that, when the time comes and we are called upon to defend ourselves against the enemy, we also will do the right thing without hesitation or doubt.

Leaders are not to be subject to the whims of the discontents of the flock, because in every group there are those who will target the leaders to take the spotlight off themselves. They demand that the leader do their will, and in the process create no end of confusion and trouble.

Government

> Do not entertain an accusation against an elder unless it is brought by two or three witnesses. (1 Timothy 5:19)

An elder who goes bad is a public matter, and the church should proceed carefully to rebuke an elder. Most of the complaints against leaders, however, come from ignorance, rebellion, and the need for a scapegoat – and should be dismissed as such. It's easy to hurl accusations against the leaders when you're sitting in the back row, but they are almost never true. Moses had continual complaints and accusations thrown against him, all undeserved. Leaders carry burdens that the members know little about – not only the commands from the Lord about things that must be done in the ministry of the church, but the problems of all the members of the church weigh on them also. Criticisms from ignorant members only make things harder for them.

> Obey your leaders and submit to their authority. They keep watch over you as men who must give an account. Obey them so that their work will be a joy, not a burden, for that would be of no advantage to you. (Hebrews 13:17)

- **Third**, Christ has given **spiritual gifts** to various members of the church. In today's churches, the subject of spiritual gifts is little understood and almost never explored. Preachers are always hammering on the subject – "everyone has a gift they should be using" – but members, though willing, have no idea how to proceed in even identifying their gift, let alone using it. And then you often have that insecure pastor who would really rather you *didn't* use your gift because it would take away from his own power and influence in the church!

The gifts are designed to distribute Christ's grace to the flock. They are channels through which the King influences and blesses his subjects from Heaven. The gifts that Christ gives to the church[2] are listed in Romans 12:6-8, 1 Corinthians 12:8-10, Ephesians 4:11, and 1

---

[2] This brings up an important point – you can't claim that every natural skill you might have is a "spiritual gift." Christ knows what his church needs, and he enables the bearer of the spiritual gift to do the work he is after. You may have a natural artistic ability; but "art" is not one of the spiritual gifts. His Word, remember, reveals the truth to us and directs the affairs of the church, not our opinions or feelings.

Government

Peter 4:10-11. A spiritual gift brings others into the presence of Christ. It makes the spiritual world of God more real to people so that they are confronted, encouraged, enabled with the presence of God in their lives. It aids in worship, the life of faith, seeing the truth of the Word, and obedient living. As you can see, the jobs of "pastor" and "teacher" are not the only means that Christ spiritually enriches his flock. It's critical for the spiritual well-being of the flock that every member does his duty and helps build Christ's Kingdom.

Failsafes

Church members often go into a panic when you tell them they have to follow the leadership of the church. Their excuse (it may just be a cover-up for an insubordinate attitude) is that the leaders are fallible too. How are we going to make sure the leaders do the right thing? What if the leaders go wrong? In other words, they don't trust anybody else's judgment except their own – especially when it comes to someone telling them what to believe or how to live.

The reason this is usually just a cover-up for their own unwillingness to follow anybody is the conclusion they inevitably draw: since it's *possible* that leaders may go wrong, then let's not have a government with *anybody* in charge. Or, let's *all* of us be in charge. Or at least make it possible for us to get rid of someone we don't like.

The Bible doesn't authorize us to throw the baby out with the bathwater. Yes, it's possible for sinful men to take a perfectly good system of church government and ruin things. But that doesn't mean we do away with church government. The Bible does give us safeguards against sinful leaders. But the Lord commanded us to *submit to his form of government*, even if we have to discipline a few people along the way who abuse the system – including the leaders.

To be a leader in the church is a sensitive and perilous role. Though we do it in humility, remembering our own weaknesses, we also must do it with the authority that Christ gave us and not let others reject our role simply because we are sinful men. It's like the policeman who stops us for speeding: we had better do what he says – the Law stands behind him and gives him his authority – even though

Government

he probably speeds occasionally too during his off hours! The teacher of the Word has his own sins (which he should be working on!), but to reject the ministry of that teacher is to reject the Lord who sent him. Nevertheless, the leader is under a double burden of his own soul as well as the souls of others.

> Not many of you should presume to be teachers, my brothers, because you know that we who teach will be judged more strictly. (James 3:1)

A real limitation in the leadership of the church is that they can't see into a person's heart as Christ can. They may think that a member is being obstinate and rebellious against the teaching of the Word, when actually that person may be struggling with the issue secretly and going to Christ about it continually. That's why leaders need to stick to their job and let Christ do his.

The options available to church leaders are limited due to their *inability to change the sinner's heart*. Even when there's sin in the church the leaders can only bring it out into the open and, if the sinner won't repent, put him out of the church. Paul told the Corinthian church to see a certain person to the door – and not to let him back in until he repented. Such a "punishment" seems light until you realize who will actually do the punishing. It's not the church's job to punish; they are simply to bring the situation out and deal with it.

> When you are assembled in the name of our Lord Jesus and I am with you in spirit, and the power of our Lord Jesus is present, hand this man over to Satan, so that the sinful nature may be destroyed and his spirit saved on the day of the Lord. (1 Corinthians 4:4-5)

You can learn the lessons of Christ the easy way or learn them the hard way. Satan is a cruel taskmaster; a rebel will wish many times, before the ordeal is over, that he had done it the easy way and submitted to the leaders of the church! And the church, in doing its duty, leaves any appropriate punishment up to God, who alone knows how to bring the sinner back to repentance.

Government

What are the failsafes that the Lord has given the church as it follows human leadership?

- *According to the Word* (*Acts 17:11*) – The Berean church checked up on even the Apostle Paul by comparing what he taught them against the Word of God. Remember that Jesus rules over us through his Word. That Word is open to anybody, from the least to the greatest. It's not the private property of the leaders of the church – as the Roman Catholics attempted to impose during the Middle Ages. Anybody with the Spirit of Christ leading him can read the Bible for himself and see what it says. If a teacher or preacher is teaching doctrine or practice that is directly contrary to the Word (and if he is, others besides yourself will see it too – be careful of being a lone ranger with zeal and no knowledge!) then he needs to be confronted and dealt with. The ultimate authority in the church is the Lord and his Word, not the human leadership.

- *Two or three witnesses* (*1 Timothy 5:19*) – The leader of a church is a natural target for discontents; he shouldn't be subject to false accusations from members who don't like the way things are going. But if a leader really has done something that needs correcting, there should be a few witnesses – more than one, so that no lone wolf can make trouble for the church – who can verify that there really is something wrong with this elder. If there was something done or said that was injurious to the flock then the witnesses will have a clear, unified testimony that will easily convince the whole assembly. Rebuking an elder is a serious matter and should be done with care and deliberation. There is proper protocol and procedure for this – it's not a time for mob rule or midnight lynchings!

- *Subject to the prophets* (*1 Corinthians 14:32*) – Those who bring the Word of God to the sheep are not free to make things up. How many leaders have felt free to add a little fire to the text to make themselves more powerful

Government

and wise in the eyes of the ignorant! But there are other saints in the assembly that have the same spirit of discernment to the true meaning of the Word as you do. If that's really what the text says, they will agree with you. But if it isn't saying that at all, they are duty bound to disagree and correct you.

- ***As I follow Christ*** *(1 Corinthians 11:1)* – Paul was filled with the reality of his calling as an Apostle; he knew the Lord assigned him the task of taking the Gospel to the Gentiles and start building churches. His back was covered by the Lord's own appointment. But he knew that he was just a man, subject to weakness and ignorance as is any man. So he counseled his students to take his ministry seriously – in so far as he himself followed Christ and followed his example. Who can argue with that? If this is what Christ said, then church members are obligated to believe it no matter who teaches it to them. If Christ commanded us to live a certain way, then we are bound to live that way also, as the leaders show us how. Their authority comes from taking Christ's mantle upon themselves and leading by his divine example.

- ***Let the spirit convict*** *(Philippians 3:15-16)* – Church members are obligated to learn and do what their leaders teach them. Their dependence on the leaders makes them vulnerable. It's that childlike dependence that makes some men giddy with power and they overstep their bounds. They go beyond their calling and demand that "their" people follow their instructions exactly, immediately, if they want their approval. But we can't police people's thoughts, their actions during the day, or their practices in the privacy of their homes. We can tell them what that Lord expects of them, but we can't change their hearts to want to live like that. As leaders we are responsible to show them the way, but we can't make them walk in it. Only the Spirit of God can change a sinner's heart to love God and want to obey him. *There is the wisdom of leadership – to know where his responsibilities end and where the Lord's work begins.*

- ***The Bride of Christ*** (*Ephesians 5:25-27*) – The last point relates to this one. The church leaders don't own the church, the members don't belong to the leaders. This is not man's kingdom. Christ bought these people with his own blood. They belong to him alone. The leaders are appointed as under-shepherds; they are only delivering a message from the Bridegroom. Once that message is delivered, it's their duty to step out of the way and let Christ deal with his Bride as he wishes. The practical side of this is seen in how church leaders "follow up" on their ministries. If they are putting themselves in Christ's place, they will follow people home and beat the sheep until people do what they want from them. But if they consider themselves only to be messengers from the Lord, they will leave obedience and sanctification in Christ's hands and timing. Instead of beating the sheep, they pray for them, counsel them, and keep teaching them with the hope that someday the Spirit will change their hearts.

- ***The three stages of Matthew 18*** – This well-known passage gives us a clear, simple procedure for dealing with any trouble maker in the church, whether he be member or leader. First, the brother or sister living in sin is approached by the person he offended. If he won't listen, then the matter goes to the church leadership – the elders, the first line of defense in the church government. At this stage everybody becomes aware that the problem really is a problem and other members agree that this person needs to repent, that it isn't just a minor spat or a person taking unnecessary offense with someone. Then if the offender won't listen to the church leadership, take it to the church level. At this point, the whole church makes it plain to the offender that this kind of behavior is injurious to the peace of the church and will not be tolerated. This procedure is both fair and merciful and, if done in the Spirit of Christ, should take care of any problem that would arise in the church – including dealing with wayward leaders.

Government

Disaster

Families have parents, governments have prime ministers and presidents, classrooms have teachers, and churches have – nobody. We all understand the importance of leadership in all aspects of life except, for some strange reason, in the church. There *we all* like to rule. Every Tom, Dick and Harry is an expert in the Bible and church doings, and they're not satisfied unless they have a (major) say in what goes on there.

If Jesus doesn't rule in his church you will have certain disaster. Ruling ourselves is the very essence of sin – it's rebellion against Christ's rule. It's the reason the world is in such a mess as it is. It's the reason God has reacted with such anger and cursed the human race with death. If church members refuse to accept the King's government – as it is revealed in his Word – they are cutting themselves off from the King and can only expect him to visit them in his wrath, with his Heavenly army behind him. The Bible makes this very plain.

> I have installed my King on Zion, my holy hill ... Therefore, you kings, be wise; be warned, you rulers of the earth. Serve the LORD with fear and rejoice with trembling. Kiss the Son, lest he be angry and you be destroyed in your way, for his wrath can flare up in a moment. Blessed are all who take refuge in him. (Psalm 6:10-12)

Many churches have no intention of submitting themselves to Christ's rule over them. They also think that they have a wonderful church going – they aren't in the least impressed with the Bible's threats and so they ignore them. They seem to be blissfully unaware that Christ has written "Ichabod" over the door of their assembly and he is no longer there among them. They are also blind to the fact, or they choose not to see, that the Mission isn't being accomplished among them – since they refuse to submit to the Word, the Spirit isn't saving them from their sin and they aren't being prepared for life in Heaven. They are earth-bound and destined to be destroyed in the end. Anarchy and lawlessness brings spiritual disaster on a church.

Government
The Churches in Revelation

Christ's government over his churches is perhaps the most obvious aspect of the seven letters. He speaks with authority; he gives them commands; he's not in the least interested in their opinions or excuses; he expects immediate results; he threatens punishment to those who don't obey him; he promises rewards to those who do his will.

He also addresses each letter to the "angel" (in Greek this word also means "messenger") of that church – perhaps a reference to the spiritual leader, or chief elder, of the church. You can see how he governs his Kingdom by sending his Word down the hierarchy and making the next level responsible to pass the Word along to lower levels and enforce that Word.

One letter in particular has a promise that, if they listen to him and obey him ("to him who overcomes and does my will to the end"), he will place them higher in the chain of command. They will be raised up in the hierarchy of his government because they proved faithful in their duties; David did the same for his loyal followers in his day. They will have "authority over the nations ... just as I have received authority from my Father." (Revelation 2:26-27) It's interesting that it doesn't promise that the church will ever become a democracy. It remains a Kingdom, though only some seem appreciate that fact now.

Summary

Jesus is building a Kingdom, not a mob that rules itself. His Kingdom has Law behind it – his Law. He expects strict and immediate obedience to his commands. Rebels must be punished or eliminated; loyal subjects will be rewarded with higher levels of responsibility. The success of the Mission depends on everyone recognizing and respecting the authority and structure of Christ's system of governing his Kingdom. It's through his government that Christ maintains justice, ensures prosperity, brings peace, provides discipline and training, and elevates his subjects to the privileges of living with God. It's time that the church recognizes her King and begins doing his will.

Service

The word "saint" has undergone a radical transformation over the centuries. In the Early Church, the word simply meant being a Christian. During the Middle Ages it changed in meaning – it referred to certain Christians who dedicated their entire lives to the work of the church: monks, priests, hermits, missionaries. Now in the Roman Catholic church a saint is someone who has dedicated their lives *and* performed one or more miracles; the process that they've invented to elevate someone to sainthood is long and complex, and requires the Pope's signature at the end.

It's unfortunate that the word has lost its original meaning, because it actually describes what every Christian believer ought to be. We are all saints, according to God's Word.

> To all in Rome who are loved by God and called to be **saints**: Grace and peace to you from God our Father and from the Lord Jesus Christ. (Romans 1:7)

The Greek word is "ἄγιος" [*hagios*] – which literally means "holy one." And we get the word "holy" from the Old Testament – the Hebrew word "קָדַשׁ" [*qadash*] which means "set apart, consecrated." The idea comes from the Temple in Jerusalem. There were items in the Temple that were to be used *only* for the service there; they were not to be used in common ways – as in someone's home. These items were "set apart, consecrated" for the service of the Temple. In other words, they were for God's use only.

This means, then, that Christians – who have been made holy – are now set apart for God's use only. They are not to live their lives for themselves, satisfying their own lusts and desires. They are to serve God in everything they do.

Service

And whatever you do, whether in word or deed, do it all in the name of the Lord Jesus, giving thanks to God the Father through him. (Colossians 3:17)

Christ is building a new Temple for God to live in – and we are that Temple. Just as David laid the plans and gathered the materials for a Temple for God's dwelling place, Jesus is building us up as "living stones" into God's eternal house. This is the reason we must be holy. We are his servants, created to be like Christ in holiness, living before God as his priests. We have no more to do with this world.

We mentioned before that many people think they "serve God" with their 15 minutes of devotions – which amounts to about 1% of their day. That's not "holy," by any stretch of the imagination.

The point of Christianity is not how *little* we can do, but how *much* we can do. We aren't called to keep our worldly lives intact and let our faith change things as little as possible. We are called to switch sides and get ready for a drastic change in our lives. "Therefore, if anyone is in Christ, he is a new creation; the old has gone, the new has come!" (2 Corinthians 5:17) Being a new creation means our lives won't look the same at all — our interests, our activities, our allegiance, our conversation, our ways and methods, will change from what describes a sinner to what describes a child of God.

Low-level Christianity

We may as well look at the problem first; some people need a lot of convincing when it comes to work. But it's good for us all to see the dangers of not being busy about the work of God.

> I went past the field of the sluggard, past the vineyard of the man who lacks judgment; thorns had come up everywhere, the ground was covered with weeds, and the stone wall was in ruins. I applied my heart to what I observed and learned a lesson from what I saw: A little sleep, a little slumber, a little folding of the hands to rest — and poverty will come on you like a bandit and scarcity like an armed man. (Proverbs 24:30-34)

Service

There really are dangers involved when we are careless and carefree about the things that God has given us to do. Too many Christians have the same attitude that the world has — I'm just going to enjoy myself, there's plenty of time to do things tomorrow — and then they get caught by circumstances with no answers and no help available *and then wonder why everything is going wrong.*

Speaking of the world, the first thing we should notice about the careless Christian is that there is very little difference between him and the unbeliever. In certain times in history there was a great deal of difference between Christians and non-Christians, because being a believer meant being persecuted. People didn't take that step lightly! But in our day physical persecution doesn't often happen in our Western culture. Being a Christian is often simply a matter of expressing some interest in the things of God, spending a little time in church, and a few other religious activities. There really isn't much that makes their lives different from the old life they used to live. It's hard to spot a Christian nowadays because they do most of the same things that the world does, they dress and look like the world does, and they have most of the same values that the world does. It's not easy to see how closely we are tied into our culture; it's almost impossible to separate ourselves from it. In fact, we think that we don't have to — we can be a follower of Christ as well as do everything that other people in our society do.

But the Bible has some things to say about that. The Apostle Paul condemns such an attitude:

> Do not be yoked together with unbelievers. For what do righteousness and wickedness have in common? Or what fellowship can light have with darkness? What harmony is there between Christ and Belial? What does a believer have in common with an unbeliever? What agreement is there between the temple of God and idols? For we are the temple of the living God. As God has said: "I will live with them and walk among them, and I will be their God, and they will be my people." "Therefore come out from them and be separate, says the Lord. Touch no unclean thing, and I will receive you."

Service

"I will be a Father to you, and you will be my sons and daughters, says the Lord Almighty." (2 Corinthians 6:14-18)

Our main characteristic should be separation from the world, not being a part of our society. People should look at us and condemn us for our separatist attitude — it should be that obvious! There are good reasons why we have little in common with them: *first*, we love the God that they hate; *second*, everything we do should be for his glory, whereas life apart from God in our world is for the devil's glory and man's personal lusts; *third*, we no longer want any of this world anyway — we have been promised a better world (Hebrews 11:16). All our efforts should be toward *that* end, not for things here. Remember the Mission?

It's unfortunate but the typical Christian has a low-level approach toward his faith. We can describe too many people in the following way:

He goes to church. This ordinarily would be wonderful, but too often people use it as the litmus test for being a believer. They are just warm bodies in the pews; they aren't there to learn anything, so don't push them with having to think too much. Therefore, most of what happens in church is of a social nature where they see their friends every week.

Going to church doesn't make someone a Christian! What do you *do* there? What have you accomplished by being there? If it weren't for the "fellowship" (we will see this in a minute) would you be as well off at home? This isn't an academic question because many people see through the emptiness of "churchianity" and stay home anyway. If all that you get done there is put in some time, going to church isn't doing for you what the Lord intended it to do.

He reads his Bible some. Surprisingly there are more than a few Christians who never read their Bibles. Most, however, will read it at least a little bit — the "devotions" that they spend a few minutes doing each day. "Reading" the Bible means to just read through a chapter or two daily. Bible study

Service

is a lost art nowadays. Strangely, we are the most educated people on the planet, yet we approach the Bible as if it's no more than a comic book — a thing to read a little while and then put aside when we are tired of reading it.

A few Christians go to Bible studies, but even there they don't actually spend much time studying the Bible itself. Usually it's just a discussion group that focuses on a particular topic (which often isn't a Bible passage but simply a current event or social issue, or often another book). And too often, even if they were given homework in which some Bible reading was necessary, they didn't do it.

He has fellowship with Christians — of sorts. Fellowship is a strange word these days. Most of what people use it to describe is their discussions with other believers. Most of those discussions, however, don't necessarily have anything to do with their faith! Christians sometimes feel uncomfortable around unbelievers (that's good!), but then they form tight groups among themselves and feel superior to those who don't go to church. They talk to each other about family and jobs and sports and social events and politics just like anybody else, often with little or no spiritual purpose beyond being Christians talking about it.

He does a little work in the church. Believers are just like anybody else these days: don't expect too much from them. The church is important to them in theory, but to expect them to lay out time and money and effort for the Lord's work turns out to be a disappointment. You can talk a few into doing something in the church, but don't ask too much and certainly not if it will cost them a lot in the long run. (There are a few exceptions, however, as in any social group where a few people seem to be a bundle of energy and volunteer spirit.) When they finally *do* something, they feel like they have done God a wonderful favor! They'll let everyone else know about it, too. (Matthew 6:1-4)

Service

He tries to curb some sins. We do have a conscience, and becoming a Christian wakes up that conscience so that it becomes more sensitive to sin. We sometimes feel bad when we hurt someone's feelings, and we are surprised at ourselves when we react so quickly in anger. These and a few other common sins are the ones that seem to impress us the most and we generally make some kind of effort to curb them. It may, however, be motivated more out of keeping our reputation up than genuine sorrow over being a sinner! And are we guilty of any other sins? Not that we are aware of (and we don't want to hear about it if we are!).

Prayer is mostly self-centered. Listen to the prayers of most Christians. Their prayers are almost always about what *they* want *from God*: physical needs, health for themselves and their friends and relatives, and not much more specific than that. They will bring "Christmas lists" to God, expecting him to give them what they want. The thought never seems to cross their minds that prayer is coming to God to find out what *he* wants *from and for them!* Many prayers aren't even very specific — just general "Lord, bless us" prayers in which nobody could really tell afterwards if God actually answered the prayer.

This is a fair description of what you will often see in today's churches; it is typical Christianity for most people. If this were pleasing to God, the Scriptures would say as much and there wouldn't be any cause for concern. But as we are about to find out, this is *not* enough — being a Christian involves far more than this life of ease that most people think it is. We have been deceived into thinking that such "Christianity" will be sufficient to get us into Heaven. We mistakenly believe that, on the day of Judgment, God will be impressed with such a record and welcome the person who lived like this.

A holy Temple

One of the most precious books in the Old Testament is the book of Leviticus. Yes, you read that right – the book you probably thought was the driest book in the Bible! One of the surprising lessons of

Service

Leviticus – one that isn't stated in so many words but is there between the lines of the entire book – is that God wants to live with his people. He came to earth to set up his throne among the Israelites. No other nation on earth had been so honored up to this time.

In Exodus and Leviticus we read about the Lord giving Moses strict instructions about how to build a Tabernacle.

> Set up the tabernacle according to the plan shown you on the mountain. (Exodus 26:30)

The point was that God has a Temple in Heaven that he lives in. He wants also to live among his people, so he gave them the blueprints to build one on earth exactly like the one in Heaven. Of course they would be using earthly materials to build it, whereas the Temple in Heaven is spiritual; but the materials used (the Lord carefully described what was to be used, and how to prepare it) would somehow symbolize the spiritual realities in Heaven's Temple. We may not understand why certain things were used, but if we could take a trip to Heaven and see the Temple there we would immediately realize why the Israelites had to use the things they did to symbolize them; the correlation between physical and spiritual would be clear.

Because of this care to build the Tabernacle in a certain way, the Israelites would know that they could indeed come to and see their God. There is only *one way* into God's presence, and the Tabernacle opened up that way to them.

According to the laws in Leviticus, there are very strict rules about how one should approach God. There are several reasons for this:

> **First**, God is holy and expects us to give him the honor due to him. For example, Isaiah was struck with the holiness of God when he saw him in his Temple in Heaven. (Isaiah 6) If God is this pure, this righteous, this full of glory and majesty, then the only conclusion we can come to is that there is nothing more important to God than holiness. We may not have been very interested in it up until now, but if we wish to have any

Service

dealings at all with this God then it's time to make holiness a priority in our lives. God is at the center, like a hub of a wheel, and the rest of us rest in him alone for our very existence.

Second, Heaven is a unique world with its spiritual peculiarities and characteristics. And now that Heaven has come down to earth in the Tabernacle, the Israelites have to learn how to live in this spiritual world. They have to learn the rules of protocol, so to speak – how to approach the King, how to present their requests to him, what kinds of things to expect from him, what his priorities are, the changes he intends to make to our world, and so on. If someone just blundered into God's presence without knowing the rules or how the game is played, he would look like a fool in front of the angels – who always stand before God's throne to serve him. (Is this perhaps what Paul means in 1 Corinthians 11:10?) He also won't get what he wants when he shows such disrespect for the King.

Third, the right of approaching God is a high privilege. Not everyone can claim the right to come close to him. We moderns are so used to treating even our rulers in a democratic way that we little appreciate how much higher God is than we are, and that we have no right to a hearing at his throne unless he extends his scepter and honors us with a command to approach him. (See the book of Esther for an example.) The priesthood symbolized the high honor and privilege of certain individuals being allowed to serve God.

So the laws of the Tabernacle give us the necessary insight about how to live with God. It's going to be a learning experience for sinners, who have been cut off from God for so long that nobody has any idea of the proper way to deal with him. Leviticus, for example, lays out complex rules for purifying sinners before approaching God. Because God is so extremely holy, there is no way we will be allowed into his presence until we cleanse ourselves with sacrifices.

Service

The laws of purification that are spelled out in Leviticus cover both the common Israelite and the priest. Both the one who comes close to God, and the one who offers sacrifices to God through the priest, must be made holy and clean for God to accept them. Read through the rituals and ceremonies for cleansing for all kinds of sin. You should get a good idea of how seriously God takes sin – no unwashed sinner will be allowed into his presence! The same is true of his Temple in Heaven. So many people think that a little sin here and there is of no importance to God. Yet things that we wouldn't have thought would make any difference to God are an offense to him. The laws cover personal hygiene, personal relationships, the houses we live in, family practices and marriages, justice in court, business practices – every aspect of our lives.

Not until we purify ourselves from all forms of sin will our worship be acceptable to him. He will not relax on that requirement; our worship, when done with sin in our hearts, is an offense to him, even if it's done according to normal procedures. He is setting down a principle here that we will see all through the Old and New Testaments – true worship is not only what we do on the physical level, but it's also a complete dedication to God in our hearts and minds and total lifestyle.

> Who may ascend the hill of the LORD? Who may stand in his holy place? He who has clean hands and a pure heart, who does not lift up his soul to an idol or swear by what is false. He will receive blessing from the LORD and vindication from God his Savior. (Psalm 24:3-5)

> Therefore, if you are offering your gift at the altar and there remember that your brother has something against you, leave your gift there in front of the altar. First go and be reconciled to your brother; then come and offer your gift. (Matthew 5:23-24)

> Come near to God and he will come near to you. Wash your hands, you sinners, and purify your hearts,

Service

you double-minded. Grieve, mourn and wail. Change your laughter to mourning and your joy to gloom. Humble yourselves before the Lord, and he will lift you up. (James 4:8-10)

The House of God

One of the aspects of the Mission of the church is that Jesus is forming *us* into a Temple where God wants to live. That thought is staggering; if Solomon struggled with the idea of the great God living in his little stone Temple, how much more should we be staggered that God would make his House out of the likes of us!

> Consequently, you are no longer foreigners and aliens, but fellow citizens with God's people and members of God's household, built on the foundation of the apostles and prophets, with Christ Jesus himself as the chief cornerstone. In him the whole building is joined together and rises to become a holy temple in the Lord. And in him you too are being built together to become a dwelling in which God lives by his Spirit. (Ephesians 2:19-22)

> Don't you know that you yourselves are God's temple and that God's Spirit lives in you? If anyone destroys God's temple, God will destroy him; for God's temple is sacred, and you are that temple. (1 Corinthians 3:16-17)

> As you come to him, the living Stone – rejected by men but chosen by God and precious to him – you also, like living stones, are being built into a spiritual house to be a holy priesthood, offering spiritual sacrifices acceptable to God through Jesus Christ. (1 Peter 2:4-5)

The goal is to *live with God*. When we become Christians we are brought directly into his presence, and there is where we will stay. As Peter says, we are living stones in the wall of this Temple that Jesus is building. We face God continually; we serve before him continually.

Service

We can no more take a vacation from the presence and service of God than one of the walls to the house you live in can take a vacation. You belong to him now.

And Jesus is careful to build this house on a secure foundation – the Bible.

> ... built on the foundation of the Apostles and Prophets, with Christ Jesus himself as the chief cornerstone. (Ephesians 2:20)

> Therefore everyone who hears these words of mine and puts them into practice is like a wise man who built his house on the rock. (Matthew 7:24)

Everything that is done in the church *will be done according to the Word of God* – if Jesus has anything to do with it. Both the Old and New Testaments describe our faith, God's Kingdom, the work of Christ, our enemies and the victory over them, and our future hope. The Bible is the blueprint for the building of the church, just as David gave blueprints (direct from God) to his son Solomon for direction on building the Temple. And just as Solomon was to follow David's directions without deviation, in the same way Jesus – and we who are his "co-laborers" – must also adhere strictly to the Word of God in the building of Christ's church.

This new Temple is a holy house where God lives. This means, as we've seen before, that our entire lives are dedicated to God's service now. Christianity is not just a matter of what little we do in church on Sundays, but changing our entire lives to serve God day and night in all our activities. The job of a Christian is the most important work that a human being could possibly be about. There is no other position in life so critical and so necessary to do. People who have high positions in society think that they are important, that the welfare of many people depends on them — but they have no concept of the staggering job facing the ordinary Christian. The world's work pales in comparison. Here is a short list of what the Bible claims is our duty under Christ's rule.

Service

- Soften the heart – *Jeremiah 17:9*
- Strengthen faith – *Hebrews 12:6*
- Become holy – *Hebrews 12:14*
- Crucify sin – *Matthew 16:24*
- Learn of God – *Colossians 1:10*
- Change the life – *John 3:3*
- Live a life of repentance and forgiveness – *Luke 18:13-14*
- Be reconciled to God – *2 Corinthians 5:20*
- Follow the ways of God – *Psalm 25:4*
- Rely on the works of God – *Psalm 111:2*
- Be a child of God – *Matthew 18:3*
- Learn the Word of God – *2 Timothy 3:14-17*
- Wean oneself from the world – *Hebrews 11:15-16*
- Spiritual duties to perform – *Ephesians 6:18; Psalm 1:2*
- Good works – *Ephesians 2:10*
- Gain assurance – *2 Corinthians 13:5*
- Relations to others – *Galatians 5:22-23*
- Build the Church – *1 Corinthians 12:7*
- Prepare for suffering – *John 15:18-21*
- Live in the grace of God – *Hebrews 4:16*
- Prepare for day of death – *Ecclesiastes 7:2*
- Prepare for day of Judgment – *Matthew 25*

Christ also refuses to have polluted servants in his service – so we have to look righteous, think righteously, and act righteously. No wonder then that so many of the passages of the New Testament hammer on this point as a crucial aspect of being a Christian.

> You were taught, with regard to your former way of life, to put off your old self, which is being corrupted by its deceitful desires; to be made new in the attitude of your minds; and to put on the new self, created to be like God in true righteousness and holiness. (Ephesians 4:22-24)
>
> Do not let any unwholesome talk come out of your mouths, but only what is helpful for building others up

Service

according to their needs, that it may benefit those who listen. And do not grieve the Holy Spirit of God, with whom you were sealed for the day of redemption. Get rid of all bitterness, rage and anger, brawling and slander, along with every form of malice. Be kind and compassionate to one another, forgiving each other, just as in Christ God forgave you. (Ephesians 4:29-32)

For you were once darkness, but now you are light in the Lord. Live as children of light (for the fruit of the light consists in all goodness, righteousness and truth) and find out what pleases the Lord. Have nothing to do with the fruitless deeds of darkness, but rather expose them. (Ephesians 5:8-11)

The Apostles were keenly aware of the new position that every Christian occupies before the throne of God. They teach us not to shame or disgrace the name of Christ with an unholy life. We are servants of the Lord now: act like it.

A Priesthood

Today's Christians probably have not thought much about what it means to live and minister in God's house. Most Christians, unfortunately, think that this talk of the Temple belongs in the Old Testament and it's not relevant to today's church scene. But they're wrong. The passages we just looked at teach us that, like it or not, you are now part of the Temple of God, with all of its rights, duties and privileges.

That means if you want to find out what those rights, duties and privileges are, you have to go back to the Old Testament and learn them! It was all spelled out there to the Israelites on a physical level (to make it easy to understand and learn) but was *intended for all believers* – including us.

One of the aspects of Temple worship that stands out prominently is the role of the priest. Peter tells us that we Christians are now priests also, serving in God's house.

Service

> But you are a chosen people, a royal priesthood, a holy nation, a people belonging to God, that you may declare the praises of him who called you out of darkness into his wonderful light. (1 Peter 2:9)

The priests, you will discover, [after they were cleansed – that was a part of their service that they were supposed to take *very* seriously!] were responsible for offering sacrifices, offering up praise, leading the worship, and declaring the blessings of God to the people. Put yourself in their position for a moment. What would it be like to offer up the same sacrifices, repeat the same prayers and ceremonies, year after year, without change? Would it become tedious? I think we can get to the heart of what motivated their service by reminding ourselves of the two greatest commandments that God gave them.

> Love the LORD your God with all your heart and with all your soul and with all your strength. (Deuteronomy 6:5)

If the priests so loved God that they were fascinated with his infinite goodness, continually preoccupied with his wisdom and works, awed with his continual presence and love, and excited with the possibilities of communion with God whenever in his presence – then their service to him never got dry or boring. It was the one bright spot in their day.

> Do not seek revenge or bear a grudge against one of your people, but love your neighbor as yourself. I am the LORD. (Leviticus 19:18)

If the priests really loved their neighbor they would take his burdens upon themselves, they would cry when their neighbor cried and rejoice when their neighbor rejoiced, they would give whatever they had and then some to help their neighbor in need, they would labor to make their neighbor greater at the cost of themselves. Their service in the Temple for the benefit of their neighbor would never be a burden but a blessed opportunity to bring joy and peace, prosperity and cleansing, to the ones they love.

Service

And that is the goal of the servants of God in the church. We are called to be priests – to worship, pray to, and listen to the Lord in his glory. We are to love him so much that worship is an opportunity to bring glory to the God we love, and to offer ourselves in his service with no reservations, nothing held back. We are called to be priests – to do whatever we can, with all the power that Christ gives us, to bring down the blessings of the treasures of Heaven to our brothers and sisters in their spiritual need.

> How lovely is your dwelling place, O LORD Almighty! My soul yearns, even faints, for the courts of the LORD; my heart and my flesh cry out for the living God. Even the sparrow has found a home, and the swallow a nest for herself, where she may have her young – a place near your altar, O LORD Almighty, my King and my God. Blessed are those who dwell in your house; they are ever praising you. (Psalm 84:1-4)

The prayers of priests

Prayer is an integral and powerful aspect of priesthood. Since we are going by the book, it shouldn't be any surprise to you to learn that God has also set the **agenda** for our prayers. We are not free to pray for anything that pops into our heads or hearts. If we're really paying attention to his Word, we will know what the Lord has given us to accomplish his Mission and we're not going to waste his time and ours praying for things to satisfy our lusts. (James 4:3) There are serious concerns in every church and individual's life. We, however, really foul things up when we always go to the throne of grace to pray for blessings of a physical nature, when God is waiting on his faithful priests to bring issues of his Kingdom to his throne!

> So do not worry, saying, 'What shall we eat?' or 'What shall we drink?' or 'What shall we wear?' For the pagans run after all these things, and your Heavenly Father knows that you need them. But seek first his kingdom and his righteousness, and all these things will be given to you as well. (Matthew 6:31-33)

Service

Again, we find the model in Solomon's day. When he finished the Temple that his father David had commissioned him to build, he brought all Israel in worship to the new house of God. (2 Chronicles 6) According to the profound wisdom that God had given him, he asked God to hear them when they brought *these* concerns to him.

- **Justice** – One of the most frustrating things to see in this world is how the wicked get what the righteous deserve, and the righteous get what the wicked deserve. Sinners get away with murder, they lie, steal, commit sexual immorality (in all of its gross forms!) and not only do they get away with it, the law of the land encourages them in it! The righteous, on the other hand, are persecuted for being righteous. This injustice is like a cancer in God's creation; it ought not to be. The saints should be offended and deeply concerned that sin goes unpunished and an upright life is despised. And the grossest injustice of history is the bad reputation that Israel's God himself has among the wicked of the earth!

  So, we pray that these wrongs may be made right – that God would protect his people and deal out justice for them, and that he might be known and glorified in the earth.

- **Defeat** – Ideally we should never lose to the Enemy. Nobody can lose if they have God behind them. The reason we succumb to the world and its temptations, our flesh's desire to respond to those temptations, and the devil's lies about the reasonableness of sin is that we've wandered away from God. Our *sins* bring us to defeat. And when a Christian is living in defeat from enemies who ought to be easy to resist, that's a shame on our profession of Christ.

  So, we pray that the Lord will surround us, live with us, and give us the resources to defeat our enemies.

- **Sustenance** – Life is very basic for most people – feed them and clothe them and they are happy. Jesus taught us

Service

that the Father will take care of our physical needs like these; we needn't worry about them *if we are seeking first the Kingdom of God. That's* our more basic need. We need spiritual bread, the water of life, the treasures of Heaven. We need forgiveness and cleansing, robes of righteousness, a holy life, strength and wisdom for the walk of faith. How can we go on without the Bread of life?

So, we ask the Father to feed our souls and trust him to take care of our other wants in this world.

- **Afflictions** – Troubles and trials come upon everyone on earth; as the Bible says, God sends both to everybody, good or bad. To a Christian, however, those afflictions are a test of character. They will bring out into the open whatever faith you may or may not have. They are opportunities to witness to the world about how the Lord provides for his people – spiritual strength to persevere under the problems of life. Even the great Apostle Paul learned that some "thorns" are best left in place as we learn to walk in God's grace.

So, we pray that the Lord might give us his strength in our weakness.

- **The alien** – God many times reminded the Israelites that they were once aliens, earlier in their history. Until God took them to the Promised Land they were slaves, with no hope and no God, living in bondage to the enemy. It's bad form to finally reach your Promised Land of blessing and peace with God and then despise those around you who aren't on your level of achievement. Our heart should go out to those who are still living in bondage and darkness. We should welcome them among us – not to remain in their sins, but be rescued and transformed as we were.

So we pray that the Lord would rescue the perishing, and would give us the grace to welcome them and give them the spiritual blessings they need.

- **War** – While God's people are still in this world, there must be war. Woe to us if we let our guard down! Our enemies are working full time to destroy us; we must therefore be continually in war mode, ready to defend ourselves against their attacks. This requires knowing our Mission, training (and lots of it!), attention to what's going on around us, respect for authority and command, immediate action in the face of battle, courage and persistence, unity of purpose and a united front against the enemy. It is time to destroy the works of the enemy.

So we pray that the Lord would arm us for battle and lead us into the fight, victorious.

- **Captivity** – Unfortunately it's human nature to learn things the hard way. If we would simply follow the Lord's will on the church and individual levels, the whole system should work and everyone would benefit. But that's not going to happen. Sinners ignore God, the wicked ignore and despise the Prophets, even God's people are wayward and refuse to follow the Lord's expressed will in his Word. So, sometimes to get our attention and forcibly bring us around to his way of doing things, he deliberately hands us over to the enemy to learn our lesson. As Proverbs says, "the kindest acts of the wicked are cruel." Satan is a cruel taskmaster. When we are thoroughly miserable in our lonely estate, when we're sick of not being part of a good church, when all within is desert and dry and there is no hope on the horizon, then – like the prodigal son – we come to our senses, humble ourselves, and plead with God to have mercy on us and restore us.

So we pray that the Lord might not leave us alone in our punishment but forgive us and bring us back into fellowship with him.

These are the issues that are on God's heart. He wants us to be concerned about the weightier matters of the Kingdom, and pray for answers that will build, sustain and protect God's Kingdom. It takes maturity to pray like this, but that's the goal of the church – to raise mature Christians.

Service

> ... until we all reach unity in the faith and in the knowledge of the Son of God and become *mature*, attaining to the whole measure of the fullness of Christ. (Ephesians 4:13)

The Churches in Revelation

If Jesus is a King, then it's assumed that we are his servants. He expects us to perform according to his expectations – to produce a profit for the Master. The churches in Asia Minor were judged by the King according to their works, just as the New Testament warns us.

> For we must all appear before the judgment seat of Christ, that each one may receive what is due him for the things done while in the body, whether good or bad. (2 Corinthians 5:10)

Two churches stand out here in Revelation. He commended the church at Thyatira for their good service.

> I know your deeds, your love and faith, your service and perseverance, and that you are now doing more than you did at first. (Revelation 2:19)

The church at Laodicea, however, didn't receive such a glowing report card from the Master.

> I know your deeds, that you are neither cold nor hot. I wish you were either one or the other! So, because you are lukewarm – neither hot nor cold – I am about to spit you out of my mouth. (Revelation 3:15-16)

One church did exactly what he told them to do – as a church, and as individual members. The other one didn't. We can ask, at this point, where are those instructions? How did they know what to do to satisfy the Master? The answer is that *the entire Bible* is Christ's instructions to his churches! We could take time out to trace these ideas here in these letters and find where they first appeared in the Bible; they really are there. It's sobering to consider that these churches were given the same instructions on how to obey Christ that we now have in our hands. How would we fare under his scrutiny?

Service

What would he say to us? Has our service to him and to our brothers in the faith been acceptable to him? Or would he have the same condemnation for us who haven't been following his instructions to the letter? He knows our deeds too; would he approve of them or not?

Summary

The ministry of the church is designed to "prepare God's people for works of service." (Ephesians 4:12) As God's people, we have been made holy – set aside for God's exclusive use. We no longer belong to ourselves. We are part of God's spiritual Temple where he lives, and must be cleansed and prepared and trained for his service. We are priests who are charged with the duties of bringing glory to God and the blessings of Heaven to our fellow Christians. Our prayers, a continual incense in the house of God, should reflect our continual desire and devotion for the building of God's Kingdom. And God will judge us according to the quality of our service to him. It's time the church took seriously its duties in the Kingdom of God.

Conclusion

Let's summarize what we've looked at so far.

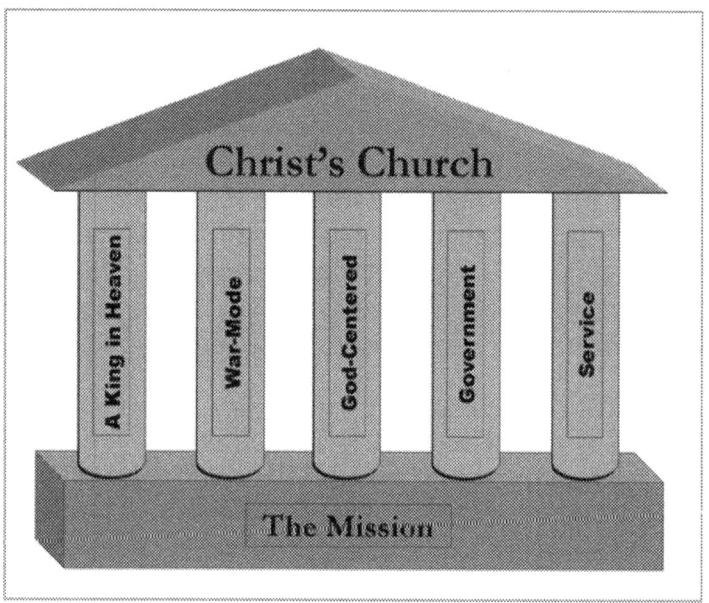

First, Jesus – being the Son of David – uses David's 5-point plan to build up the Church, the Kingdom of God. Because we have gotten ourselves in such a mess, and we can't fix things ourselves, we need a strong leader who will create a nation around the presence and power of God and heal us of our problems.

Second, the **Mission** that Jesus wants to accomplish is to create a holy people who serve God continually in his Temple. That will require cleansing our hearts and minds as well as our lives of all traces of sin and rebellion against God. It will require training and educating us in the ways of God's spiritual world. This Mission will guide everything Jesus does in the church; it defines not only the goal but the means of reaching that goal.

Third, there are five pillars that must be in place for a strong and spiritually healthy church. They include:

Conclusion

- **A King in Heaven** – Jesus has gone on to Heaven to build his Kingdom from *there* – it's to be a spiritual Kingdom, firmly based on spiritual treasures. The Old Testament taught us the principles of the Kingdom in physical terms, but now the time has come to build it with spiritual materials, as the New Testament directs us. Christ works with us through his Word and Spirit as he rules from his throne there.

- **War mode** – The time has come to deal with our enemies conclusively. The three enemies – the world and its temptations, our own flesh that responds to the world, and the devil who deceives us into sin without taking seriously the consequences – are not going to rest. Jesus' great conquest is to deal a death blow against these enemies, and we are to arm ourselves for the battle and follow him.

- **A God-centered ministry** – The time has come to push man out of the spotlight and focus our minds and hearts on God. The purpose of the entire Bible is to reveal God to us – his nature, his glory, his works and ways. These are the things that will save us; God himself is our treasure in Heaven. The entire ministry of the church needs to be founded on the need to know God.

- **A Government** – Jesus ascended the throne of Heaven as Creation's King. It's time the church came before his throne and bowed down to him. He intends to set up a kingdom of righteousness, justice, blessing, peace and prosperity. He assigns his subordinates to rule in his name. The church is a hierarchy with Christ at the top, and the rest of the system carrying out his orders. This is the only form of government that will successfully accomplish Christ's Mission.

- **A life of Service** – Christ made us to be spiritual stones in the Temple of God, continually in God's presence and serving him alone. This means that we have become holy – set aside for God's use only. And he made us to be priests,

Conclusion

worshiping God in an acceptable way and serving our brothers and sisters in need with the treasures of Heaven.

When David finally handed over the Kingdom to his son Solomon, he had achieved all that the Lord wanted to do for the nation Israel. He alone in Israel's history had done the necessary things to bring Israel back to God as a holy nation. God had given him insight into the secret of building the nation, and David's heart was in it. Israel, in Solomon's day, had prosperity and power and peace like she had never had in her past and never would again.

In other words, these principles work. Jesus is using these same five pillars to build his Church – with the result that the children of God will enjoy unimaginable blessing, power, peace and prosperity both now and in eternity. His heart is in this project; he willingly set aside his glory to come do this great work in us.

His disciples remembered that it is written: "Zeal for your house will consume me." (John 2:17)

Our task is to learn and understand what Jesus is doing, and change our work in the church to conform to his plan. A half-hearted attempt won't work. If we use only a few of these principles, the house cannot stand – we have to become skilled at applying the whole counsel of God to the needs of the church. Like David, we must become ruthless in our determination to bring order out of the chaos of our present situation. People's souls are at stake.

It's time his churches become aware of the great Builder's methods and goals and build his church in his way.

Notes

www.ingramcontent.com/pod-product-compliance
Lightning Source LLC
Chambersburg PA
CBHW020902090426
42736CB00008B/470